THE LOVE IN OUR TEARS

NATHANIEL EMBERS

EAST STREAM GROUP, LLC
Weaverville, NC

THE LOVE IN OUR TEARS
Copyright © 2016 by Nathaniel Embers.

All rights reserved. Printed in the United States of America. No part of this book may be used or reproduced in any manner whatsoever without written permission except in the case of brief quotations embodied in critical articles or reviews.

This book is a work of fiction. Names, characters, businesses, organizations, places, events and incidents either are the product of the author's imagination or are used fictitiously. Any resemblance to actual persons, living or dead, events, or locales is entirely coincidental.

For information contact/visit :
support@eaststreamgroup.com
http://www.eaststreamstudio.com

Book and Cover design by East Stream Studio, Weaverville, NC, 28787
Book Formatting by Derek Murphy @Creativindie
ISBN: 978-0-9910342-3-9 Hardcover

First Edition: January 2017 (Revised)

10 9 8 7 6 5 4 3 2 1

READ THIS FIRST

The Love in Our Tears was first birthed in the minds of the creators of the Web series When Fact Met Fiction.

Nathaniel Embers is the fictional alter-ego of one of the show's lead characters, Jon Frank. See About the Writer at the end of the book for even more details regarding the origins of this novella and it's award-winning roots in Southern Appalachia.

Also, if you haven't discovered it yet, you can watch all the episodes of the romantic comedy When Fact Met Fiction anytime on YouTube and Vimeo.

CHAPTER 1

"Would Madame care to sniff the cap?" – Uncle Hoyt

It wasn't Elenora Reese's first journey to the mountains, but their varied and verdant greens still surprised her. While summer came a little later here, it also tended to linger awhile into the autumn. The drive down 81 from New York, usually beautiful in the late summer, was about as boring as it could be, with most of Pennsylvania and Virginia doused in relentless rain that only abated when she reached Bristol.

Her first view of the southern Blue Ridge Mountains was cloudless and startling. Even though she had visited often as a little girl with her mother, she had been too young to really appreciate their quiet grandeur. Instead of rising up to impose their majesty like the Rockies, they rested on the landscape like a welcoming friend or relative. The lush trees were spread across them like an inviting quilt of deciduous and coniferous patches over a rumpled bed. She rolled down the window to enjoy the sweet, cool air. She was so enamored with the beauty that she nearly missed her turn at the bottom of the mountain. Her destination only had one main road in or out. Of course, there were numerous smaller roads and cow paths that led over the ridges, but the natives of Wayah, North Carolina knew outsiders only came in by the main road, a long twisting route that first climbed and then descended, serpentining on itself more than a dozen times.

Ele, already nursing a headache and slight indigestion, was on the brink of carsickness when at last she crested Higgins Gap, the last hill before town. She pulled the rented Subaru over on a wide place at the roadside, a patch she assumed was used in daytime by tourists to take photos, and on Saturday nights by teenage Lotharios trying to make Monday-morning school-gossip headlines. Leaning on the car's fender, she sipped a 7-Up and surveyed the town of Wayah stretching over the valley like a cookie sheet of Americana. It had grown up on the limited flat spaces above the flood plain of the deep, wide, rocky Cane River, which from this height was a shiny green ribbon draped on the landscape.

When Ele's stomach had settled somewhat, she returned to the Subaru and descended the last mile into town. There was Main Street, the courthouse, the maple-enclosed square, and the dominating steeple over Wayah First Baptist Church. A cafe clung to the square's south side, just up from a small movie theater that looked much as it did on opening day in the 1930s. Several shops and boutiques huddled along the side streets like the crowd waiting for a parade: a hair salon and barber shop, exclusive of each other; a hardware, an antique store, and a music store whose display window proudly boasted a chorus line of banjos and fiddles. Absent were the myriad subway tracks and busy multi-lane streets that were a constant in Manhattan.

Just at town's edge Ele turned a sharp right onto 17W, a narrow two-lane road that followed the river northward. She remembered this part of the drive from her childhood. The sun was just setting to the left over the nearby ridge, but its light still shone brightly on the farms and pastures to the right across the river. The sunbeams danced and sparkled like strobe lights between the leafy trees along the ridge, and the breeze through her open window seemed to whisper, "Welcome home, Ele, we missed you." Ele knew, of course, that only Uncle Hoyt would've really missed her, and Aunt Estus if she were still alive.

Two years ago Hoyt and Estus had decided to put their house on the market, so her aunt had called Ele to see if she would come down and pick out any furniture or knick-knacks she would like to keep. They hadn't spoken in over a year before that call. Nearly twenty years had passed since Ele had visited, and she couldn't remember any item special to her. No, she told Aunt Estus, they should sell whatever they wanted to help cover any expenses. That was the last conversation Ele was to have with Estus; two days later her aunt collapsed while packing china in the kitchen and was gone.

Ele's guilt was a brick on her heart, but her life in the city gripped like a vice. She was successful, but only just, and she wanted more. No, that wasn't entirely true; she needed to be more honest with herself. Sure, there had been upcoming tax deadlines that alone might have prohibited her from attending the funeral.

But honestly, she was ashamed. Ashamed of what she had become in spite of the light her aunt and uncle had shone ahead for her. To Ele, Aunt Estus was an elegant lady-in-waiting with simple Southern values like home, hard work, and love for her community, and Sir Uncle Hoyt was Ele's knight and protector. But Ele had stained herself in myriad ways over many years, and she couldn't bear for them to discover the dirty knees under their little princess's white lace-trimmed petticoat.

She gave tax deadlines and work as her excuse, and her uncle said he understood, she shouldn't beat herself up about it, and that her aunt would have been upset if Ele had made a fuss.

Now, two years later, when Ele received a phone call from the attorney representing her uncle, she expected to hear morbid news.

Instead, he explained that Ele had been designated executor of the Canby estate and Uncle Hoyt had requested she come help him close up the house and move into assisted living. Her uncle, the lawyer continued, had been diagnosed with early-onset dementia and was determined to manage his own disposition while he still had the wit and will to do so.

Ele tendered her resignation, giving Uncle Hoyt as the excuse. The firm couldn't expect her to quit because of her other situation, and of course they wouldn't fire her. Yet it just felt better not to discuss her own future with her superiors, even though they had been reasonably kind to her all this time. She just wasn't ready to verbalize the big personal news yet. After all, it would reveal itself in a handful of months anyway.

Ele's first real glimpse of the Canby house was almost two miles down 17W. It was a large but simple Victorian, complete with a turret and wraparound porch, perched on the hill across a low, grassy field that flattened out next to the river. As a girl Ele thought it was a castle, and asked her mom if Uncle Hoyt was a king – or maybe a knight! – and if he could protect them from trolls and dragons. Her mom replied that yes, Uncle Hoyt was indeed a knight who had slain many dragons in his lifetime.   The structure was originally a boarding-house adjacent to the stretch of river where the ferry had crossed. River ferry service ceased in the early twentieth century with the advent of automobiles to the region, but there had never been a traffic bridge laid across the Cane here. Instead, a swinging footbridge constructed of cable and wood spanned the banks about fifteen feet above the tumbling water. As a little girl, Ele adored tromping across its swaying planks, much to her mother's constant terror. Her uncle was notorious for encouraging Ele to cross it with an endless list of small tasks, one after the other. This way she would always have an excuse: "But Uncle Hoyt made me get the mail, Uncle Hoyt told me to check for duck eggs, Uncle Hoyt asked me if the river was still flowing the same way on both sides." Despite its precarious appearance, the footbridge was expertly built and well-maintained, and its unchanging presence every summer of her childhood never failed to fill Ele with comfortable security.

She passed the house, watching for the turn onto an ugly concrete-and-steel car bridge another mile up 17W. Built by the WPA in the thirties, it was sturdy as the day it was built and had survived numerous floods and city councils lobbying to have it replaced. The Subaru bounced pleasantly over the bridge and flat ruts of the single-lane road beyond.

Memories flooded back of walking this shaded driveway, feeling between her toes the clover growing down the middle and under her bare feet the cold brown clay. The car wheels glided over the smoothly-packed surface that must not have been graveled since then.

In a moment the house came back into view ahead. Its wooden sign had weathered to gray, but the letters WAYAH INN Est. 1895 were bright and welcoming. Suspended underneath from two tiny chains was a smaller shingle that read, Hoyt Canby VMD. Ele recalled Uncle Hoyt saying many times that VMD was special, that only a few distinguished veterinarians in the country could put those letters after their name. He would declare, "A University of Pennsylvania School of Veterinary Medicine graduate is a Johns-Hopkins doctor for animals."

She pulled the car just past the front stairs of the porch and got out. The rumbling river, a scant hundred yards down the hill, seemed to applaud her arrival and she almost felt the place sigh with relief at her presence. She imagined the Inn would seem smaller; yet here it was, a large and imposing dowager at the ball. The lady, as gray and weathered as the sign, could still turn heads and get her dance card filled. Sharply-angled gables showed a century of wear, but the ornate trim with its viney curls and scrolls was a lovely tiara over the tall luminous windows with shutters standing guard at the sides. The turret commanded the house like a sentinel watching over the river and surrounding environs, and behind its slender windowpanes was her favorite room, which youthful Ele had considered her own even though she shared it with her mother. It presented a fantastic view of the river, footbridge, and pasture, and she would perch on the window seat, reading or coloring horses and flowers while keeping an eye out for new boarders. She even had a quiver of paper airplanes ready to defend her tower if any kids arrived.

Snuggled under the turret was the massive porch that wrapped around the right of the house and boasted antique rockers, Adirondack chairs, and a chipped white porch swing. The flagstones up to the four broad steps, while cracked in a few places, had recently been weeded and cleaned. The steps were glossy with fresh paint, and she noticed a fairly new handrail added to the left side.

The front door banged open and a tall gangly man with a shock of cottony white hair clambered down the steps to greet her in his usual way, "Elly, Elly, Oxen-Free!" Uncle Hoyt grabbed her up in a joyous hug, lifting her off the ground and squeezing her in close. She giggled, and he set her down but still held her. She snuggled against his cardigan and relished forgotten smells of pipe smoke and wet dog. Her tears gushed unexpectedly, and he shushed her and rubbed the back of her hair.

Ele sobbed, "I am so sorry, Uncle Hoyt. Please forgive me for not coming and for not calling and for not being here."

He pushed her back and tilted his head down to make eye contact. "Oh shut up, you big baby, you're making a scene and scaring the animals," he chided.

She laughed at his brusque manner and punched him softly in the arm. "No, you shut up!" she cried, wiping tears with the back of her hand. "Just for that, you can carry up my stuff."

He exclaimed in mock disbelief, "What? You're staying here?

What do you think this is, a boarding-house for ugly people? I won't have it! They'll shut us down and I'll have to move out of state."

She gave him a crooked smile and pointed at the Subaru's trunk. He put up both hands in surrender. In spite of her victory, Ele helped carry some of the luggage.

"I thought you might be hungry, so I picked up some dinner from town," Hoyt said over his shoulder. "Grace at the cafe makes a mean country-style steak and mashed potatoes. It's nowhere near what your aunt could whip up, but it eats good and keeps the kitchen clean."

"Sounds awesome. Let's just get this stuff upstairs and we'll dig in."

Uncle Hoyt pushed the screen door open with a toe and the pair trekked up the broad main stairway, bags and trunks jammed under their arms and hanging awkwardly from their hands. The stairs bisected the Inn's interior like a spine. Made from rich dark oak, with a navy-and-gold tapestry runner cascaded down the center, their foot-worn surfaces had been witness to thousands of political, culinary, romantic, and devious plots. The banister was a thick affair that had seen its share of kids' sliding backsides – and occasionally, Ele knew, her uncle's when her aunt wasn't around. Ele paused for a moment before following Hoyt upward, enjoying the familiar pop and creak of each tread. The stairs terminated at the top in a T, the right and left landings u-turning to hallways down either side.

Hoyt wheeled around the right banister newel, bumping down the narrow open walkway and through the second door. He placed her bags on the window seat inside and Ele flopped the rest of her parcels on the low cannonball-poster bed. Her uncle asked, "Well? Is this okay? I hope so. I couldn't remember if this or the square one on the other side was your room. I had Boone make up both rooms so you could choose. I like this one because it has the turret with the best view of the river – and it looks out directly at the footbridge."

Ele kindly refrained from mentioning this sign of her uncle's waning memory. "It's perfect, Uncle Hoyt, really. Let me clean up a little and I'll be right down to supper."

"Okay. Hey, I had Boone put some little soaps in the bathroom," her uncle said. "They're turtles, I remember how you like turtles." Ah, so her uncle hadn't forgotten everything. He patted his shirt and pants pockets. "Okay. See you downstairs in a bit, then." He turned and shut the dark paneled door behind him, muttering to himself down the hall and stairs.

Ele sighed and looked around. Her room was exactly as she remembered it, albeit a bit smaller. On the right was the ancient cedar wardrobe, on the left two yellow Queen Anne chairs and various ornate lamps and side tables. The small mantelpiece was flanked by two dusty brass sconces, and over the bed were two tin-types of her ancestors hunched in gilded frames, the same ones her uncle had once convinced her were actually trolls. The floor-to-ceiling antique blue damask wallpaper was almost overpowering, and Ele was grateful the large windows and billowy lace curtains lightened the space.

Ele pulled the wardrobe knob and it opened with a loud pop and creak. The familiar gust of old wood and mothballs assailed her nose. Ele had a special fondness for this wardrobe. Often as a little girl she would hide in the bottom so long she fell asleep, and her mother would let her nap until she woke.

She closed the door and turned around to survey her reflection in the oblong cheval mirror. Her eyes lingered on the physical differences between now and the last time she was in this room. Back then she was a spindly nine-year-old with big front teeth, overly-large blue eyes, and dirty blonde curls that laughed at any brush daring to approach them. The teeth she had grown into, thankfully, but not the eyes, which still appeared slightly larger than her face was supposed to carry. Her hair remained blonde but had traveled through many levels on the spectrum, including shoe-polish black. It now steadied at a high blonde with curls softened into large waves.

Ele ran her hands over her t-shirt, turning slightly to press the width of her hips and assess her figure. In ninth grade she, as her mother observed one morning, had "popped," stopping just this side of voluptuous. She had always been athletic but the rapid physical changes of puberty frustrated her, so she turned to academic studies. Her personality in high school changed rapidly as well, from quietly friendly and a bit nerdy to fun-loving party girl with a different boy chasing her every few months. As crazy as her Friday nights and long New York summers were, however, she didn't let them affect her schoolwork.

After high school, Ele accepted scholarships in economics and business and graduated cum laude from CUNY. When the investment firm on Seventh Avenue hired her, they obviously appreciated the value of her brains – but she was never entirely certain her looks weren't a major draw for a practice heavy in the "old lech" department. Ah well, she thought, I suppose in my present condition that doesn't matter anymore.

Ele changed into a fresh tee and sweatpants for dinner and descended to the dining room. The table was set with plastic cutlery and two styrofoam containers of food, and she flopped into the nearest chair. Uncle Hoyt, who was staring out the window, turned to her with a smile.

"I have taken the liberty of selecting our wine this evening," he announced, placing a bottle of Cheerwine across his arm sommelier-fashion. "Would Madame care to sniff the cap? I assure you it is an excellent week, from the finest vineyards in Salisbury."

"Oh, my goodness," Ele exclaimed, a hand at her bosom, "so fancy! I'm not sure I can afford this place."

Their drinks poured, Uncle Hoyt seated himself and stuffed a paper napkin under his collar. Ele cut a chunk of country-style steak, swirled it around in the potatoes and gravy, and pushed the huge bite into her mouth. "Ohhhhhh, that is so good. You can't grow good meat and gravy like this north of Virginia."

They spent the rest of the meal making small talk about her trip. Uncle Hoyt picked up the dinner leavings and placed them in the trash. "Ele, it's still light out if you care to take a walk. I usually turn in about now, you know. My medicine, it makes me sleepy."

"Will you be all right? I mean…?" She didn't know how to delicately approach the subject. She'd read up on early-onset dementia and guessed his problem wasn't medicine but sundowning. She wondered, was Uncle Hoyt even aware that it happened? Uncle Hoyt studied her for a moment. As if reading her thoughts, he said, "Listen, Ele, I am not ignorant of my condition. I have an MD from UPenn, even if it is for pets and cows and such. Yes, sometimes I sundown, and sometimes I sunrise, and sometimes I shouldn't trust my farts so much. But I assure you, at this point it's still early on – early enough to know my limitations, mostly. I'll be fine – and when I'm not, you'll know. Fair enough?" He tilted his head in that way that always told Ele he was serious.

She sighed. "Fair enough, Uncle Hoyt. I'm going to take a walk and try to undo about twenty pounds of supper. Is there still a trail along the river?"

"All the way down to the tobacco barn." She hugged him and he patted and rubbed her back. "I'm really glad you're here, Elly-bean. Truly."

"Me too, Uncle Hoyt, me too."

CHAPTER 2

"I always have, Ele." – Boone

From the Inn porch Ele could see her old friend the footbridge on the right, the river road on the left. She couldn't resist one bouncy jog over the footbridge's rough boards, but once on the other side, the main road looked as pleasant as a parking lot. Backtracking, Ele walked briskly toward the river road.

The path along the river was really just a continuation of the drive leading to the house. Perhaps it had been a road in horse-and-buggy days, but by today's standards it was barely one lane. All the same, Ele noted, someone kept the path in marvelous shape. No invasive weeds or stray overhanging branches broke the thoroughfare, and even downed limbs were scarce. The early-evening summer sun was nearly behind the ridge, and edges of twilight gray approached. It was that golden time, quiet and still, yet abuzz with birds and insects and the river's soft roar.

The Cane was wide and deep. Murky, fast-moving stretches were interrupted by boulders and slender playful falls pouring into churning pools. The green water slithered through pastures that once produced tobacco crops that many families in this area had depended on for their living. When smoking dropped out of favor, tobacco growers down east turned to soy and other crops. Here those types of crops simply required more land than a man could effectively profit from, so many fields were converted to pastureland or sold off for summer homes, organic micro-farms, and community gardens. Ele had written a college paper on the regional economic impact of this transition, yet never thought about it again until now. She wondered how this valley might have turned out if the location had been uglier and tourism absent. As it was now, there were two or three small-scale manufacturing plants on the edges of town, but it was the seasonal influx of visitors, followed by somewhat-local skiing in the winter, that kept this community from financial ruin. It had certainly kept Wayah Inn in business.

Ele's ponderings carried her almost a half-mile along the river when she noticed a fly fisherman on the edge of a quiet pool. She continued her stroll until she was almost parallel to the man, the entire time watching him tilt the rod back and forth in that curious ten-and-two dance. The line swirled about and the lure brushed the water's surface just at the pool's opposite edge. The fisherman was a maestro conducting an insect symphony for his piscine audience, and Ele found herself mesmerized by the show. Her eyes roved from the lure's precise darting dance on the sunlit pool, up the glistening line, and back down the waving rod to the man himself.

Ele couldn't see his face but noticed dark hair under his ball cap. He wore an olive-green fishing vest over a pale green t-shirt, and no waders, just work boots and cargo shorts. He again orchestrated the pole's arc, and she watched the music play in his biceps and forearms. His muscles were lean and smooth, and he had the uneven tan of a man whose work kept him outdoors a lot. Ele, entranced, observed the man step slowly to avoid jostling the water, all the while performing his precise fly-rod prestidigitation.

As the man inched forward a branch blocked Ele's view, so she glanced up and reached to move it. Suddenly her left foot slipped and she grasped the slender limb for balance. It immediately snapped and she fell backward – off the embankment and into the river.

The cold made her immediately breathless, and she was deafened by growling water rushing around her. The current rolled her over and over, flailing her on rocks, but somehow she managed to point her head skyward and spring up from the riverbed. Just as she breached the surface, however, the current drove her into a boulder and forced her under once more. The surprise shocked her and she gulped a mouthful of water.

At the moment she began to panic and fling her arms about, two other arms encircled her from behind and raised her to the surface again. She was hauled out and over to the shore, coughing and choking, her unseen savior backing up the bank.

Her breath eased as they stopped halfway, and she looked backward to see the beautiful fisherman holding her. He smiled, his perfect teeth encircled by a dark, close-trimmed beard. His eyes were the darkest brown she had ever seen; if they weren't so close, she would've thought they were black.

"Are you all right?" the man asked.

"Yeah, I think so," Ele gasped. "Th-thank you." She turned to lie back against him again. It was then she saw his hands were clasping her across the chest.

At that moment the man also noticed the placement of his hands and quickly let go with an embarrassed smile. "Uh, sorry."

"Oh, no, that's quite all right," Ele replied quickly, smoothing back her sopping hair and wiping water from her face. "Again, thank you. I really should look where I'm going. I'm Ele, by the way." She extended a hand.

"Yes. Oh, I'm Boone. Boone Buchanan," he replied and again shotgunned her with that fantastic smile. He took the proffered hand. Ele smiled back and wondered at the gentle, callused strength she felt in his grip.

"Here, let me help you the rest of the way up." He braced himself and pulled her up the bank. He held out his other hand to steady her torso, but thought better of its placement and allowed it to hover instead. They met at the top and suddenly stood facing each other.

Boone was easily six-foot three, and Ele cried unexpectedly up at him, "Oh, your tackle! You've lost your tackle! I am so sorry! Was it expensive? Please allow me to pay for it."

Boone looked down on her and smiled again. "It's quite all right; I'm sure I will find it later. Now, let me walk you back to Doctor Canby's."

"How did you know I was staying there?"

"You're Elenora, Hoyt's niece. He said you were coming. I had hoped to see you tomorrow when I came to breakfast, but this way was much more interesting."

"Now I really am embarrassed," said Ele. "The first time we meet and I'm flopping about like a seal. Truth is, here lately I'm not the most graceful thing on the planet."

"I really wouldn't know," he said, "but I hope I can rescue you again if that's the case."

Ele blushed. "Well, I was beginning to work up a sweat, so at least now I can skip the shower. You don't need to walk me – I know the way back. Thanks anyway." She made a silly face, clapped her hands together, turned upstream – then abruptly spun and pointed the other direction. "I'm, um, that way. Nice to meet you, Boone." Somehow she couldn't resist the urge to shake his hand again, to have some small bit of further physical contact.

She took a step toward him and immediately hooked her sandal in an unearthed tree root, flying forward into Boone's arms. Once again, she found herself looking up into those marvelous dark eyes. But then she felt stabbing pain in her chest. Her mouth opened and her oversized blue eyes became even larger.

Boone, who had begun chuckling, abruptly stopped. "What is it?" he asked, trying unsuccessfully to step back from her.

"DON'T MOVE!" she cried. Her lips trembled. "Ow ow OW help me please oh help help help!" They both looked down between them. Connecting Ele's right breast to Boone's vest was a finely tied, elk-hair caddisfly fishing lure. The fake insect was still attached to the vest, but the long, curving fishhook was buried deep in the folds of Ele's t-shirt and soft flesh underneath.

Boone quickly but deftly slid off the vest. Ele held it to herself as her right hand shook with the urge to touch the lure. "What'll we do?" she cried.

Boone took her hand and guided her quickly down the path back to the house. After a few eternal minutes, Boone led her around the side of the porch and opened the door to her uncle's vet surgery.

He motioned for Ele to get up on the table while opening cabinets and drawers with pointed certainty. After scrubbing his hands and pulling on surgical gloves, he turned to the table and assembled the necessary supplies. Only when Boone was prepared to proceed did he pause and look into Ele's eyes. She nodded her silent permission for him to continue.

He said apologetically, "The doc has some lidocaine, but it's locked up."

"Just do it. Whatever you need to do."

Boone produced a pair of scissors. With mechanical precision, he snipped away the fabric of Ele's t-shirt to bare the sports bra underneath. He carefully cut away a small square of the bra material to expose the wound. He bent close to Ele's cleavage and expertly examined the hook's entrance and exit. The barb had, thankfully, passed through the flesh and was fully emerged, and Boone sighed with relief that he wouldn't have to cut down to it.

"Here goes. Are you sure you don't want me to get the lidocaine? Hoyt would be okay with me waking him to get the key."

"Please, just get it out!" Ele closed her eyes and bit down, tears pouring from embarrassment and pain.

Boone sighed and set to work. Since this was a vet's office, tools for removing nails and wire were readily at hand. He snipped off the barb and dropped it into the basin. With just a moment's nervous pause, Boone gently gripped Ele's pierced breast and used sterile pliers to slide the remainder back out, heedless of her sharp yelp. He tossed the fly in the basin, cleaned the wound, and placed two butterfly bandages to close the holes and stop the bleeding. Even in her pain, Ele couldn't help but note how well Boone had completed the entire operation.

"I hope you've had a tetanus shot. If not, I'm sure Doc can help you tomorrow."

"No!" Ele said sharply. "We are not telling Uncle Hoyt any of this. As far as he's concerned this never happened. I mean it, Boone. Promise me." She took his arm and turned him, repeating, "Promise me."

"Okay, I promise."

She slid off the table and headed to the door that led into the rest of the house. Then she looked back. He was collecting the evidence and removing the trash. "Thank you, Boone. But I mean it - not a word. I expect you to keep your promise."

She left the room and never heard his soft reply, "I always have, Ele."

CHAPTER 3

"Is this every morning?" – Ele

Ele's sleep was restless and full of strange dreams. In one she was hanging from an apple tree and looking at a boy with big dark eyes. Dangling from a limb, she was terrified of falling, but the boy said, "Let go, Ele, it's okay. I've got you." She let go and plunged deep into water where she was promptly hauled up on a fishing line and held aloft like a prize trout. She spun around and saw Boone. He whispered, "I've got you."

The startled awake and sat up. The dawn air was cool, but the light was fuzzy pink that promised another warm day. Her chest was sore but not as much as she expected; Boone's ministrations had done surprisingly well. She gathered some clothes and walked down the hall to the bathroom.

The soap and steaming hot water washed her mind clear of the strange dream. She toweled off and slipped into jeans, sandals, and a white floral peasant blouse, then wiped the mirror down with her hand and stared at her face. Just then the nausea rose up and she barely made it to the toilet. Afterward she rested her head on her forearms. A sharp knock on the door jolted her.

"Are you okay, Ele?" It was Boone's voice. What was he doing here? She snapped, "I'm fine! Go away!" She heard receding footsteps and the thump-thump of boots on the stairs. She sighed and reached up to hit the handle and flush away the damage. Hopefully the nausea would only last a few more months. She had prescription Phenergan for these moments, but that was in her room miles away down the hall.

Why had she snapped off at Boone? What was he doing here anyway? And what time was it? One thing was for sure, Ele decided, the answers would not be found embracing this commode. She stood, took a sip of water, swirled it around, spit it out. Wiping her mouth on the back of her hand, she opened the door and made her way down to the kitchen. Boone was gone. Calling for Uncle Hoyt yielded no response.

"First things first. Coffee, coffee, coffee. Must have coffee." Lighting the gas burner and settling the kettle on its blue flame, Ele rummaged unsuccessfully for a can of coffee. Flipping the burner back off, she ran both hands through her damp curly locks and grunted softly. "Keys, keys, keys. Must find keys."

Then she heard scratching. Her eyes squinted as she focused on locating the sound. Scratch, scratch. It was coming from the kitchen door. Without considering what might be on the other side, she flung the door open to find a dog. It was a large, fluffy, peach-colored dog with pointed ears and a long bushy tail. It immediately stood on its hind legs and placed the front ones on Ele's waist, wagging its tail and panting happily up at her. The dog wore a harness and tiny backpack, which was odd enough. But the truly odd thing about the dog was the long leash that led from the dog's harness to the smiling naked figure of Uncle Hoyt. His face was bright from the morning sun, and he wasn't smiling at Ele but at something out of her view. In his hand was a brown bag and cup carrier with three steaming coffees. Ele stammered, "Uncle Hoyt…" but stopped when Boone turned the corner and walked straight up to the doctor.

"Good morning, Hoyt. I see you got breakfast." Boone disconnected the leash from Hoyt's waist and knelt in front of the dog, who had dropped down off Ele and jogged to Boone, tail whipping joyfully. "Good boy, Peachy." He coiled the leash neatly and slid it into the little backpack. "Head on back to town. Go on, now." Peachy looked back at Ele as if to verify she had things in hand here, then sprinted down the drive.

Ele and Boone turned toward Hoyt, who said, "Oh yes, breakfast. We were out of coffee." He handed the food off to Ele and moved past her into the kitchen.

"Hoyt," said Boone, "why don't you get dressed for your appointments, and I'll take your coffee and biscuits into the surgery for you." Hoyt nodded his assent and went down a hall just off the kitchen to his room.

Ele glared at Boone. "Is this every morning?" she asked as they seated themselves at the scratched farmhouse table.

"No," Boone replied, sliding a coffee over to her, "some mornings he doesn't get dressed at all."

She placed her hands on her hips. "What I mean is, is this what he does all the time? Is he safe going into town – like that – by himself?"

"Well, you see…people around here love your uncle dearly. As you know, he's always been a little eccentric anyway. So when the dementia came along, they were already kind of accustomed to his ways. And Peachy there, he's the town dog but loves Dr. Canby in particular. He's taken care of Peachy since he was a pup, so I guess now he figures Hoyt's the pup and Peachy takes care of him. If Doc gets to wandering aimlessly in town, someone just whistles for Peachy, ties him to the harness, and tells Peachy to take Dr. Canby home. Most times I'm never too far away so I check on him throughout the day, and when I'm not at a hired job I try to help in the surgery."

In light of yesterday's medical procedure, the revelation that Boone had been working with her uncle didn't surprise Ele. She sipped her coffee and relished its caffeinated glory. "So you live nearby? I mean, if someone had to be rescued or something."

The old ladderback chair creaked as Boone shifted to point toward a south window. "Oh, yeah. I'm right down at the end of the road there on the edge of the pasture. If you look out the window of your room, you can see my room. I like to read, so I always have a light on at night. The river prevents me from hearing a human voice, but you can ring the big dinner bell in the yard. I'll hear that. Cell phones don't work so well here, but you can have that number too. If you want." His eyebrows raised expectantly, but Ele ignored the comment and pretended to overlook the hurt on his face. He changed the subject.

"I'm heading into town to pick up some stuff at the hardware. You want to come? I mean, if you need anything too," he stammered.

Ele wasn't certain how to respond to this boyish behavior. Most men either left her alone, intimidated by her beauty – or came at her guns a-blazing. She didn't know where to place Boone on that spectrum. Anyway, letting herself consider an attraction to Boone was pointless, because she knew how things would end up. And then there was Mike.

She hadn't spoken with Mike since she arrived. But after their suspicions were confirmed...well, all the future plans had to change, didn't they? When they met, it was clear she should keep things professional, but she gave in to the raw mutual attraction. It wasn't love, merely need. Neither one expected to have to make a big plan, but the test result was clear. Now there would be a big plan; she was still figuring out the particulars on her own. He wasn't happy about that, but he hadn't called her so she assumed he was respecting her wishes until she returned.

The entire time Ele's mind had been drifting, Boone had talked on about places he had to stop and items he needed. She blinked a few times and sputtered, "Oh I'm sorry, Boone, I was off in another world. Sure, I'll go along, just let me get ready." She slid the chair back and took a long pull off her coffee. "Be right back."

"Okay," Boone said, jerking a thumb toward the surgery, "I'll just check on the doc while I'm waiting."

Ele started to sprint up the stairs, but the dizziness was immediate, so she settled for a slow jog. She put her hand to her forehead. Should she take some medicine with her? What kind of things would they be doing? "Oh, crap, Ele, it's just a trip to town. Get a grip, girl." She considered taking her purse but didn't want to look too "city." A lonely wallet seemed weird, and she didn't want to have to tote it anyway, so she settled for cramming some twenties and her driver's license in her jean pocket. She started for the door, stopped, and turned around to swap her sandals for low-top hiking shoes.

CHAPTER 4

"Of course, Miss Reese. I give my word." -J. Higgins, Esq.

In a moment Ele was back downstairs and approaching the surgery door, behind which she heard unfamiliar voices. The surgery must have a patient. She hesitated at the door, wondering if she should enter. Uncle Hoyt had always been liberal about Ele being in surgery with him, so he probably wouldn't mind. Besides, Boone was in there and she wanted to meet some of the townsfolk anyway. She pushed open the door and entered, expecting to see a dog or cat, or maybe even a goat or some other small livestock. Instead she was greeted with the strange sight of two men, one of them enormous and clad in old-fashioned overalls, the other sitting on the surgery table with a fat stick protruding from his scalp.

"Ele! Come on in." Uncle Hoyt's voice was chipper and casual despite the horrifying situation on his table. "This is Arbuckle," he motioned towards the thick, muscular man who sported a thick, black beard and a big white smile, "and this young man on the table is Squirrel." Ele was not overly squeamish, but her sour stomach rebelled at the sight of her uncle's patient. "Squirrel here has found himself in quite the predicament," Uncle Hoyt explained. "Arbuckle was recounting the accident to Boone and me. Go on, Arb, you were saying something about firewood."

The big man, who easily topped two hundred sixty pounds, placed his thumbs under his overall straps and proceeded. "Well, like I was a-sayin,' me and Squirrel was a-gatherin' wood for the boiler – er, is it okay to talk about things, you know...?" He looked at the doctor and Boone while nodding his head in Ele's direction. Both men nodded back in approval, so Arbuckle continued. "Okay, so we was unloadin' some wood for the boiler up at the site. It's the last batch that's got to be ready for Saturday and all. Me and Squirrel had us a rhythm a-goin,' tossin' and stackin' the logs. All a-sudden, Squirrel sneezes after I'd already tossed this big ol' piece in the air. It caught him right across the noggin and down he went." Arbuckle pointed at Squirrel's head. "That limb there snapped off it and the log kept on a-rollin.' Now you know he won't go to nobody but you, Doc, so here we are."

While Arbuckle had been telling his tale, Ele had been marveling at the fluid precision of Boone and her uncle addressing the wound. Like a well-tuned machine, they passed instruments, gauze, and tubes back and forth. Her uncle would whisper to Boone or point out something, never loud enough to interrupt Arbuckle's tale. In three short minutes, the stick had been extracted, the wound cleaned, stitched, and bandaged. But the most astounding part, at least to Ele, was Squirrel never made a sound, nor did he wince or even sharply draw his breath.

She couldn't resist asking, "Doesn't that hurt, Squirrel?"

Arbuckle replied, "Oh, he don't speak, ma'am. Leastways not words conversational-like. Never has."

Her uncle said as he finished the wrapping, "What Arbuckle hasn't told you, my dear niece, is even though Squirrel here isn't very loquacious, he is an excellent mimic. Squirrel, would you mind demonstrating a song sparrow for Ele?" Immediately, Squirrel produced a perfect imitation of the bird. Ele smiled with surprise and pleasure. Squirrel, obviously encouraged by such an attractive audience, proceeded to volunteer a variety of other bird and animal noises.

Ele glanced from Squirrel to Boone, shaking her head. "That is absolutely amazing!" she said, laughing. "Wow." Squirrel grinned proudly.

"Okay, boys, I think we are all done here," Hoyt said as he snapped off his gloves. "Keep it clean and dry, Squirrel, and come back in a week to get those stitches out."

"Here, Doc, I brought some of this down with me." Arbuckle produced a pint jar from his overall pocket. "I hope it's enough." Ele could see clear liquid, the contents obvious to her. "If'n that ain't, I'll give you another on Saturday at the festival."

"That'll be fine, Arb, that will be just fine." Hoyt took the jar and held it up to the light. "Magnificent."

Both men nodded to Ele as they exited the surgery. "Nice to meet you, ma'am," Arbuckle added as he closed the door.

"Boone, never mind about cleaning," said Uncle Hoyt. "I've got this. You take this girl into town and show her around."

Boone opened the door for Ele and followed her out. They made their way to Boone's pickup, a walnut brown, nineteen seventy-nine Ford. It had seen not just better days but weeks, and Ele was skeptical about climbing in the cab.

"You'll have to get in the driver's side and slide over. The passenger door is jammed," Boone said, unembarrassed.

Ele walked around the truck and peered at the bed. The passenger side had obviously experienced some kind of significant collision. The panel was crumpled in, a round aftermarket taillight was precariously mounted on top instead of embedded in the proper cavity, and the tailgate was missing entirely. Fearing a nasty cut to go along with the previous evening's wound, Ele kept her hands off. After all, a girl could test her tetanus resistance only so much. Boone yanked the driver door open and Ele scrambled into the cab.

The bench seat's passenger side was threadbare and full of holes. Settling there, Ele was promptly and uncomfortably prodded by the springs. She shifted, trying to find a perch providing the least springy metal assault to her thighs and backside.

"The middle has more cushion if you want to slide over this way," said Boone.

Visions of redneck romance sprang to Ele's mind. "No, thanks...I'm fine," she replied. Plus, she didn't want to push her resolve by sitting in such close proximity to Boone. She was here for business, not silly romance. She'd had enough of that here lately. But more importantly, she had to consider her condition.

"Just don't lean against the door," Boone warned. "It's stuck but that doesn't mean it won't fly open if we hit a rut." Ele pursed her lips and braced a hand each on the dash and seat beside her. Boone said, "We need to stop by my house before we head into town. I have to take Momma to the cafe. She's working lunch today."

They turned left instead of back toward the main road, traveling on the narrow river drive Ele had walked yesterday. The wide pasture to their left was dotted with a few cattle and their calves. Barely visible at the pasture's far end was a small, one-level house surrounded by a huddle of pines. Ele exclaimed, "Is that your house? When I was a kid, no one lived there, so I used it as a playhouse. I set up all my dolls and made food for them on an old wood stove. There was a broken-down cradle I would put them all to sleep in. Sometimes kids would come to the Inn and we played until the lightning bugs came out or Aunt Estus rang the dinner bell."

"I know," Boone whispered.

"Wow, I had just about forgotten that," she continued. "There was a little girl who came every year. Funny, I can't remember her name. She had a fat brother and a vicious Dachshund. Oh, and one year we had a Chinese family with about fifteen kids."

"They were Japanese. And eight kids," said Boone quietly.

"Oh, and there was this one boy. What was his name? The only kid who could outrun, out-climb, and out-jump me. Oh, what was his name?" Ele rubbed her forehead.

"Moses." Boone replied.

"Yes! That's it! He was here every year. His parents lived in town or somewhere and brought him out to play. I thought he was so cute. Well, not when I was little, but when I got older, yeah. I think that was right before we stopped coming. I was nine, I think? He had a big mop of curly black hair. I dared him to jump off the tobacco barn into the river. He slipped and caught a nail on the way down."

Boone winced visibly, but Ele wasn't looking.

"Poor guy, ripped his side from waist to shoulder. Uncle Hoyt sewed him up, gave him a tetanus booster just in case, and promised to keep it quiet. I guess Moses confessed, though, because I never saw him again that summer. Or maybe he was pissed at me. It was all so long ago, I barely remember. I wonder what happened to him."

"The world," said Boone sadly.

"What? Did you say something? I'm sorry. I have just been prattling along. Please forgive me."

"Of course."

In a moment they passed the embankment where Ele had fallen in, and they shared a light chuckle. Just beyond, they encountered Arbuckle and Squirrel walking the road. Boone pulled to the right and the two pairs exchanged waves.

Ele observed, "Now there's an odd couple. Do you know them well?"

"As well as anyone can, I guess. They're my brothers."

Ele wasn't sure how to reply, and then they were turning into the drive adjacent to Boone's house. The limbs of a triple-trunk river birch stretched over the ivy-covered yard that led right up to the foundation. This close Ele could see the house was tiny and old, but also that it was in the process of being restored. Pieces of siding had been replaced and the roof was a checkerboard of mismatched shingle repairs. Along one end of the sagging porch, a hanging row of Christmas ferns and brilliant red impatiens swung in the breeze, shading an antique rocker and a decrepit love seat whose arms were black with stains. Leaning on one side of the house was a small stack of new pressure-treated lumber and two sawhorses.

Boone pulled the door handle as he threw his weight against the truck door. "I'll only be a minute." He took the three porch steps in one leap and entered the open door of the house. Ele strained to hear the voices inside, but the sound was muffled by walls and distance. Boone's brothers arrived in the yard and Squirrel grinned at Ele from under the gauze taped to his forehead. Just inside the doorway a clear voice rang out, "You boys get my step-stool for the truck. Boone, don't forget my extry tank. Come on now, I ain't gonner be late 'cause of ya'll lollygaggin.' Del's gotta get to her appointment and Law knows she's got to do everthin' she can to keep them babies!"

Ele heard obedient replies from the boys. Squirrel grabbed a heavy wooden stool from the porch and placed it at the back of the truck, followed by Arbuckle with cushions from the love seat. Boone came last with a slim oxygen tank and hoses, setting them in the bed just behind the cab. As he turned to back to the house Ele called out, "I can slide over or sit in the back. I don't mind." Boone motioned for her to stay put.

A rotund woman in a floral-print dress emerged from the house. Supported on all sides by her sons – Boone on her right arm, Arbuckle her left, with Squirrel following with his extended hands ready to lend support – the woman gingerly descended the three steps and paused at the bottom to catch her breath. She crossed to the truck and propped herself against the hood. The boys released her but stayed close. She shuffled around to the window and said, "You Hoyt Canby's niece, ain't you? Law, Law, you turned plumb purty. Need some more meat on you, but I reckon I can fix that at the cafe."

Boone said, "Ele, this is my momma, Bura Buchanan."

Ele began to reply but Bura nodded toward the back of the truck. In one smooth motion of practiced delicacy, the boys guided her up the stool, across the truck bed, and on the cushions against the cab. Arbuckle and Squirrel sat down as well, taking care to avoid the rusted side of the bed. Bura placed the oxygen tubes in her nose and settled back with a loud sigh. Then she banged on the metal. "Let's go, we're burnin' daylight."

The truck backtracked to the ugly bridge, made a left onto 17W, and soon entered the heart of town. Although it was only eleven in the morning, the town was bustling. A gang of children on bicycles streamed down the hill toward the square. A work crew was setting up a stage and decorations for some sort of celebration. Boone explained it was for the Annual Shelton County Canning Festival. "It's the last hurrah of summer here," he continued, "even though it's still August. When September comes, most of the Florida people go back and we start getting the leaf-lookers, so it's one of the few times we get to be just us natives. Let our hair down, so to speak."

"Sounds fun!"

"It usually is," he replied. "They have games, fireworks, horseshoes, some dancing. More food than a man can hold, with the exception of Arbuckle. I believe he can out-eat any man alive. He can certainly out-drink them."

They pulled in front of the corner of a long two-story structure containing the county license-plate office and the Town Square Cafe. Ele climbed out after Boone and watched the perfect reversal of the sons helping their mother out of the truck – a task the men handled, Ele noticed, with loving dignity. The group entered the cafe to a chorus of salutations from a few late breakfast patrons. Bura met each one with a smile, maybe a jesting insult, and always an inquiry after the health of each customer's kin. Eventually she made her way behind the counter and shuffled to a young woman whom Ele assumed was Del due to the enormous size of her belly. She estimated Del to be maybe all of nineteen. Del stretched her back while waddling over to share a side-hug with Bura.

"Arby, you walk this girl up to her car. Careful she don't trip or she's a- liable to pop wide open and them twins'll come a-shootin' out all over the square." She kissed Del on the forehead and turned to her tasks. Draping a wide yellow apron over her head, she took a seat behind the counter. Del left amid the chatter of customers' goodbyes.

Bura announced, "Ya'll, this is ol' Hoyt Canby's niece, Elenora. Ya'll remember when she used to come in here, don'tcha? How long you stayin' with us, hon?"

"Oh, not long I'm afraid. I have to be back in a month or two at the most." Ele hesitated, then offered as explanation, "Work." Everyone accepted this with nods and return comments of "Know how that is" and "Well, enjoy yourself while you're here."

Ele couldn't help but notice a few sets of eyes drifting between her and Boone, and she felt her cheeks flush a little. Turning to Boone, she said, "So, I have some things to see to. I can meet you back here in a couple of hours, or I can just walk back home."

"No, here's fine," he replied, flashing that tremendous smile again. Ele's blush deepened when she noticed a tiny dimple under Boone's right eye just above his short beard.

Waving at Bura, Ele stepped out the cafe door and proceeded around the left side of the square. She located the office of Higgins & McCanless, Attorneys at Law and glanced over her shoulder before entering the air-conditioned reception area. There was no receptionist at the desk to greet her.

"Take a seat, I'll be right with you," called a deep baritone voice from the back. A man sporting a tweed coat and diagonal-striped tie emerged and Ele stood to shake his hand.

"Elenora Reese. You called a couple of weeks ago concerning my uncle, Hoyt Canby?"

"Yes, of course. I'm John Higgins, Dr. Canby's attorney. Come back here where we can talk." He hacked a cough and produced a pack of cigarettes, politely offering her one which she declined. Placing the cigarette between his lips, he walked toward the back, patting his sport coat pockets. They arrived at a stale, cramped office, where he gestured to a chair. He gave up the hunt for matches and tucked the unlit cigarette back in his pocket, much to Ele's relief; she hadn't yet determined how to politely ask him not to smoke.

"Miss Reese, I understand you have some questions for me. Your uncle asked me to call you, knowing you'd be willing to come under 'legal' circumstances. Of course, usually I'm bound to confidentiality by attorney-client privilege, but Hoyt has given me permission to share with you the particulars of his situation. So I'm going to lay it out straight for you.

"As you know, your uncle is in the early stages of dementia. And as you've probably already observed, he can come and go anytime, more often in the morning and evening. These spells can last ten minutes, an hour, or even two, and Doc Henry says it's likely he doesn't remember them. Hoyt's strong as a plow mule and will likely outlive me and you both, and right now, he's mostly fine up here," Mr. Higgins said, tapping his temple with a ball-point pen, "but who knows how long that will last? Doc Henry also says these things are progressive, and Hoyt'll need full-time care possibly as early as next spring. That's when things get harder. So here we are."

The doctor stood, strode over to a file cabinet, pulled out a folder, and handed it to Ele. "Hoyt's one of my best friends, Elenora. I've played poker with him every Saturday night and sat one pew behind him every Sunday morning for thirty years. This is hard for him, but he's never been a prideful man. Only things he's ever been overly proud of were you and Estus. Even your Ma didn't hold his heart like you do. Hoyt considers you his daughter, just in case you weren't aware. Did you know when your Ma turned up pregnant, he offered to adopt you? She refused of course, but…"

Ele wiped away sudden tears and looked down at the folder. "What's this?"

"That, young lady, is everything. Hoyt had me do his will and all the paperwork. Your uncle has given you ownership of the Inn, the acreage, the veterinary practice, and a substantial amount of money. You are now a wealthy woman. Now, if you like you can sell the property and head back to New York, and Hoyt assures me he is fine with that. In fact, he asked me to tell you all this instead of him so you could think about it by yourself without pressure from him or anyone else."

Ele jumped up, slammed the folder down on the desk, and shrieked, "Well, dammit!" She burst out crying in a gushing fit of snot and tears.

"Good heavens, Miss Reese! I didn't expect that kind of reaction." Mr. Higgins reached out as if to console her but stepped back again, not certain what to do with this bawling woman.

"Great, just great," Ele chuckled mirthlessly through her tears. "That's just…" She put a hand on her head and paced the room, then gave that up to slide down the wall into a crouch on the floor. The doctor offered some Kleenex; she jerked out half a dozen, wiping and blowing while she tried to calm herself. "Mr. Higgins, may I tell you something? I'm not your client, but I've just got to tell someone. You have to give me your word Uncle Hoyt – and anybody else for that matter – will never find out."

"Of course, Miss Reese. I give my word."

And she told him everything.

CHAPTER 5

"Shh, Hoyt, we'll find it." – Boone

Two hours later, Ele exited Parker's Real Estate on Baird Street and walked two blocks back to the town square. She glanced at the cafe and at her watch before taking a seat on a bench in the square's grassy center. Standing guard over her was the pockmarked statue of Grady Shelton, the frontiersman who first settled this valley, and for whom the county was named. According to the plaque, which Ele read idly as she enjoyed the breeze across her face, "Grady Shelton was Murdered by Cherokee in 1811. Mr. Shelton's Head was Discovered on This Spot, the Rest of His Remains Having Been Consumed by Wild Hogs." Slightly nauseated by this historical information, Ele slid down the bench closer to the Town Square Cafe.

Ele stared up into the trees, musing over all that had happened the past few days. Despite the cheerfully warm midday, Ele felt troubled by the way she had left things with Mike, so she decided to call him.

He didn't answer, which wasn't surprising given his strenuous work schedule, and she left a voicemail. "Hey Mike, it's me. I'm sorry I haven't called. I'm under a lot of pressure. Well, you knew that, I guess. The vomiting is pretty bad in the morning, and the headaches seem a little more frequent, but I guess it'll get worse before it gets better. Ha!

Oh, something I just remembered: Please reserve St. Marks instead of that church on Laramie. I know it's short notice, but hopefully they'll understand. I'll contact the caterer and the flower people tomorrow, just to be certain they're ready in time. Call me later. Again, I'm sorry."

Ele hung up the phone and ran a hand through her hair, clutching it back in a ball to let the breeze cool her neck. She blew out a long breath and rubbed her eyes with the heel of her hand. Stretching languidly, she opened her eyes to find Boone standing in front of her. He had a peculiar look on his face. How much of that had he heard, Ele wondered?

"You ready?" Boone asked. She accepted his proffered hand, but dropped it as soon as she stood up. They walked silently toward his truck.

Halfway across the grassy square, Ele noticed three elderly women making their way to a group of benches just ahead. Something about them held her attention, and their physical details began to emerge as they came closer. The tallest woman was heavyset and pale-skinned, her whitish hair sporting blonde highlights. The middle woman had an aquiline nose, warm olive skin, an hourglass figure, and ash-brown hair with bright white streaks. The last woman was the most striking; she was short, wiry, with Asian features and coal-black hair and eyes. While the other two women shuffled along, carefully measuring their steps, her gait was small, light, dainty. The trio found their bench, but made no conversation. They appeared to be waiting for something – or someone, perhaps.

When she was almost ten paces from the ladies, they all turned to her and smiled. The act so startled her that she stopped. Then she realized they weren't noticing her, but Boone.

Boone smiled back at the ladies, and then at Ele, adding to her confusion. He began to sidle past. "Um, could you…wait here for just a bit?" he asked, motioning toward the ladies. Ele nodded and watched him approach them.

Then he did a curious thing. Kneeling in front of the three, he began speaking, first to the white-haired woman, then to the others in turn. Whereas before they seemed stony and quiet, now they were energetically conversing with Boone. It took Ele a moment to realize each lady was speaking a different language. Even more surprising, Boone was responding to each in her own tongue, rapidly and fluidly shifting between languages like pouring water from a pitcher. One of the ladies told a joke and Boone translated it into the other two's languages. Each lady waited respectfully, smirking until the final one had heard it; then all four roared with laughter. He leaned over to receive a hug and kiss on the cheek from each lady, followed by some palsied sweet-old-lady hand-holding. As Boone stood to return to Ele, she received a final surprise when all three women shifted to English and began their own conversation.

"How?" Ele gasped. Boone shrugged. "You speak four languages?"

"Well, actually I speak five. Mrs Cardozo was Portuguese, but she died last year. She wasn't part of the War Brides, though," he said nonchalantly.

"War Brides?" asked?Ele.?

"Yeah, that's what we call them – the town does, I mean. Their husbands fought in the war, but for the other side, so we say War Brides because it's nicer than calling them the Axis. You know: Germany, Italy, Japan," he chuckled slightly. "They like hearing their native tongues. It makes them feel more at home, I guess."?

The rest of the walk to Boone's truck was silent, Ele's thoughts flying from her awe at Boone's linguistic skills, to her stunned disbelief at having inherited all her uncle's worldly goods – and landing, of course, on her absolutely honest conversation with John Higgins, Attorney-at-Law.

The silence continued on the ride back to the Inn until Boone spoke up. "Um, is everything okay?" He glanced at her and back at the road.

"No, not really. I just wish…never mind." Their eyes met for a moment before Ele turned to look out her window. "Hey, what's that up there? I don't think I noticed it before. See it? The big bare patch on the top of that mountain."

"That's Balsam Bald."

"Bald? Like a man?"

"Yeah, some folks say they formed naturally, others think they were man-made for cattle and such. The forest just never reclaimed them, too high up I guess. It's beautiful up there this time of year, if a little chilly." Abruptly, he swung the truck to the right and turned onto a narrow side road.

"Whoa! What's going on?" Ele cried and braced herself on the door frame.

"You'll see," Boone replied cryptically. He half-smiled and pushed his cap back, draping his right hand over the steering wheel. The road to the bald was, to put it mildly, unimproved. Although Boone tried to dodge the major ruts scarring the road, Ele felt like she was sliding up and down a washboard.

Once they had to wait for a bear and two cubs to meander back into the woods after they loped into the truck's path. It was Ele's first experience with large wildlife beyond the Central Park Zoo, but what truly amazed her was Boone's behavior. Here was a mountain man who had probably seen a lifetime of forest creatures, and was also a genius who spoke five languages – and yet he was just as childlike as she about the bears.

The drive took about forty-five minutes and ended at a large, flat dirt area that had seen its share of parked cars and trucks. Ele followed Boone out of the cab and immediately felt the promised chill. She rubbed her arms, and Boone stepped closer and reached around her into the cab, their bodies and faces almost touching. Boone looked straight into her eyes, and for a moment she gazed into those dark pools, feeling his breath on her cheek and lips.

He broke the moment, however, and handed her a flannel work shirt. "It's worn but clean." She slipped it on and shoved her hands into her pockets. "C'mon, I want to show you something," he said.

Boone stepped over a stile in the rotting split-rail fence. He extended his hand; Ele took it and followed. This time he continued to hold her hand up the hill. His strides were much longer than hers, but she allowed herself to be pulled a little, not wanting him to let go just yet. He grinned back at her and she looked down in embarrassment.

"Hey, what is this spot on the ground?" Ele asked. She stopped, letting Boone's hand drop. She pushed the hair back off her face, cursing the loss of her hairband somewhere in the day. They both looked down at a patch of blackened earth at her feet. The dark burn radiated out in spidery tentacles from a central hub. Around the circumference and along the tendrils, tiny white flowers grew among the luminous green grass.

Boone said, "That's a lightning strike. The flowers don't really have a name – one time I tried to look them up. I guess they only grow here. The grass is brighter green because of how the lightning alters the soil. But hey, that's nothing. Come with me."

He eagerly took her hand and guided her to a hulking boulder in the field's center. He hopped on the rock and pulled her up to him. He gestured out over the wide grassy expanse, and she gazed in awe at the dozens of such strike areas, each tendril intersecting with another in zany mockery of a road map, each strike a small town of verdant grass and tiny pale flowers. The wind began to blow just a bit and Ele reached up to pull her hair out of her face again. Simultaneously

Boone reached up to brush the errant strands back. Their hands met in a clumsy knock, then Ele dropped her arm and allowed Boone to continue. She looked away while he entwined his fingers in her hair and began to knead it softly. His touch was so intense, so strong, that Ele was terrified to look at him. Instead she touched his other hand tentatively, squeezing one of his fingers between hers.

Boone sighed and slowly, gently slid his hand out of her hair. He looked at the sky and observed softly, "It'll be getting on toward supper soon. We should head back and check on Hoyt."

"Sure, of course." Abruptly Ele sat down and scooted off the rock. Boone leapt off the edge and landed gently, like an acrobat. "There was a time I would have done that too," Ele observed. "And probably a handstand at the end," she laughed.

"Oh, I know," he said under his breath, smiling.

The ride down the mountain seemed shorter but no less jarring. Ele mentally replayed the afternoon, kicking herself for not kissing him, then convincing herself she was relieved she didn't. She considered her life so far, and suspected Boone deserved better. Besides, she had only a few weeks before she had to get back. Any longer and her secret would be out. Boone just couldn't be a part of the choices she had to make from here on.

They met Uncle Hoyt halfway down 17W to the Inn. He was tied to Peachy and had a chicken under one arm and an umbrella hooked over the other wrist. His attire consisted only of muck boots and a butcher's apron. Boone eased the truck up beside the walking pair. Peachy's tongue lolled to one side as he looked up, but he continued, stalwart in his appointed duty as guardian and guide.

"Good evening, Hoyt. How's it going?" Boone asked in greeting.

"Oh, I was just getting some chicken for dinner tonight. Thought I'd cook it, and maybe some carrots and potatoes. Would you like that, Ele?"

She looked from her uncle to Boone, who nodded almost

imperceptibly to say, Go along with it. She replied brightly, "That sounds delicious. Can I help? You know I like to cook."

"Sure...I need to find your aunt's recipe for it. I know it's out here somewhere. She gave it to me as the shopping list and I dropped it on the way to town. I had it in my pocket. Here, let me check again." He shifted the chicken, who flopped contentedly in its warm armpit roost. He slid the apron aside and began to pat his skin. "I seemed to have misplaced my pants. Where are my pants? I can't cook without pants on – your aunt would kill me. She won't even let me in the kitchen barefoot! Lost the recipe, and now my pants too? I'm a goner, Ele, a goner!"

Boone shifted the truck into park and hit the door with his shoulder. He lifted the chicken from Hoyt and set it on the ground, where it squawked at the push of his boot and ran off.

Hoyt stared timorously into Boone's face. "Boone? Where's the recipe? I've got to have it. It was her mother's!"

"Shh, Hoyt, we'll find it," Boone soothed as he untied Peachy and commanded him to run back to town. "Just climb into the cab."

Hoyt protested, "No! I have to find it. I have to."

Boone patted his arm. "Okay, okay. Ele, can you drive a stick?" She shook her head. He climbed back in, shut off the engine, and motioned for her to come take her uncle's other arm. They continued the trip on foot, Hoyt between them. After a bit, Hoyt stopped talking and seemed content to just walk quietly.

Back at the Inn, Boone led Hoyt to his room while Ele waited in the hallway. In a moment, Boone emerged and closed the door quietly.

Ele said, "Thank you, Boone. I don't know what I would have done if you hadn't been here tonight."

"It's really no trouble. I've been here every evening since he started acting like this. It'll be okay now – he'll sleep the rest of the night."

They stood in silence until Ele realized she was blocking Boone's exit. She stepped to the left and he made his way to the side door, then paused to look back at her. He nodded once, like mountain people do, and opened the door.

"Boone?"

"Yes?"

"Do you think maybe you could...stay for a little while? I could make tea, maybe a sandwich. We could...talk some?" Her request hung naked in the air.

He studied her long enough to deepen the sensation of nakedness. "No," he stated carefully. "But I'm just right down the pasture. Ring the bell if something happens."

She bit her lip and gave him her best "I need help" look, the one that usually worked. But he nodded once more and closed the door without glancing back.

She waited, staring at nothing in particular, hoping he would change his mind. In a bit she heard his truck rumble by, but it continued steadily past the Inn. She resisted running to the door and looking out, knowing that would be admitting she was desperate. Maybe she could ring the bell, pretend her uncle had awakened? Machinations of that sort worked in the past; would they work on Boone? But she didn't want to win him that way.

Wait – did she want to win him? No. Maybe. Yes? No. And not like that, manipulating him. That road ended with too many problems and heartaches. Ele knew Boone wanted her, that he could be another conquest. She had disposed of so many men that way. Maybe Boone was timber and stone on the outside, but she could tell inside he was fragile as a dry leaf. It was this juxtaposition of strength and fragility that made him so attractive.

Oh crap, she did want him. And not as a trophy, as a man. "I have the worst timing in the world. Dammit, Boone, why couldn't I have met you years ago?"

She rolled her eyes toward the ceiling. "Mom, I need you. Why didn't I listen? Why did you leave me? I need you!" She plunked down on the floor, holding her head and letting the tears fall.

CHAPTER 6

"Oh, Uncle Hoyt, I am so messed up..." – Ele

Ele's sleep was again fraught with dreams, this time of her mother. Ele had loved her mother like no one else. She was a short, wispy woman with long spirally curls much like Ele's, but where Ele had a good smile, her mother's overtook and encompassed her whole being. Joy was her name, and it fit so aptly that even her older brother Hoyt never gave her a nickname. It was impossible to remain sad when she was around, because a moment with her was like suddenly waking up and realizing it was Christmas. Hoyt adored his baby sister and provoked her to squealings of laughter that invariably ended with gasps, snortlings, and a bit of peeing. And he never judged Joy, not even when she showed up at his and Estus' door, hugely pregnant and entirely destitute. Estus and Hoyt had taken her in until she had Elenora, and then staked her some money to find her way in the City. She repaid them with summer visits, bringing the springy, wonder-eyed Ele for Hoyt to spoil endlessly.

When Ele was nine, Joy completed a nursing degree and poured herself into the care of others, so much so that she couldn't find enough time off to visit North Carolina anymore. Later, Ele entered the teen years and fun summers in the country became less important than late nights with her posse of wild high-school friends. Then, with the grace of a guillotine, her world shattered. Joy collapsed at the hospital. That morning, Ele had listened to a voicemail from her mother that she had to work a double shift that evening; at noon Ele was on the subway home, wracked with shaking fits and stunned thoughts. It was one month after her eighteenth birthday, four months before her high-school graduation. Nothing had ever again filled that hole of Joy in Ele's heart.

She climbed out of bed and made her way down the hall to the bathroom. The nausea hadn't hit yet, but it was definitely on deck, waving to the fans. "Might as well get this over with," She muttered, flipping up the seat and kneeling. She slipped a hairband off of her wrist and tied her hair back, wincing at the tightness. She didn't have to wait long for the heaves, which arrived each dawn like the morning paper. Glad it was just a little this time. She stood, cleaned up, and made her way downstairs. At least Boone wasn't here again.

Ele found coffee brewed, and toast, butter, and jelly on the table snuggled against the jug of milk. She thought about Boone again and recalled what he said about the light in his window. She wondered if she would be able to see his house this morning, maybe the truck out front. She wanted to apologize for her behavior last night. She must have seemed like a desperate floozy, begging Boone to stay like that.

On the way to the front porch, she passed Uncle Hoyt's door and softly knocked. It eased open, but his bed was empty. Remembering the previous day's events, she walked anxiously back to the kitchen door and opened it to the blue light of morning. Heavy fog lay low over the pasture and trees much like cotton across a carding paddle. She had no hope of seeing Boone's house, but she could just make out a fuzzy glow of light in the field. Something comfortable and secure settled in her heart.

Ele was turning back inside when she saw movement in the corner of her eye. A cow? No, a human shape. Boone? The nebulous figure, just beyond sight in the pasture, had spiky projections above and to the side, and occasionally she could see glints of reflected light.

Suddenly, the blanket of foggy silence was rent by the loud cacophony of a bagpipe blaring out music fit only for Scottish ears. Ele made her way down the steps and across the front lawn, where dewy grass slid and caught between her bare toes. Her city feet winced and rolled on the gravel as she crossed the driveway and slipped up to the pasture fence.

There, resplendent in all his Highland glory, was her Uncle Hoyt. He blew his song on the pipes, blissfully unaware of anything else. He wore an elongated, wedge-shaped hat with a crease in the top and trailing ribbons down its back. His waist was girded with a broad black leather belt and pouch, which Ele assumed would normally hold up a kilt. Her uncle did sport a pair of knee-high stockings and brogues, but his attire abruptly ended there. He faced the river to play his jaunty tune, unaware of Ele standing mesmerized by the whole affair.

She noticed someone else arrive from down-pasture. It was Boone. He didn't wear any piping attire, just his usual jeans and flannel button-down over a t-shirt, but he approached Hoyt, ceremoniously saluted, and took up position to Hoyt's left.

A moment later, a jumble of huge black figures began shifting ponderously through the fog. Ele smiled when she realized it was Uncle Hoyt's cattle. The cows and their calves milled about the duo, entranced with the little concert, placidly chewing their cuds. Ele counted at least a dozen cows forming a neat company in front of the comic pair and adding an occasional moo to the proceedings. She leaned on the fence post and placed her chin in her palm. Soon Peachy came running and tail-wagging among the throng. He sat at attention next to Uncle Hoyt, who continued to play as Boone stepped forward to examine the cattle one by one. He checked ears, eyes, withers, barrels and pin bones, giving each bovine lady a gentle slap to send her back out to pasture. When all was done, a good ten minutes later, Hoyt ceased playing and turned toward the house.

"Oh, hello, Ele. Good morning." Uncle Hoyt reached out and caressed her face with a warm, rough hand. "Hungry? I know I am. Boone!"

Boone turned toward them and made his way to the fence.

Hoyt asked, "Fancy whipping us up some of your momma's pancakes? You want some, Ele?" She nodded enthusiastically; her empty stomach needed something and pancakes sounded perfect. "Great! I'll clean up in the surgery while you and Boone get everything together." He turned nakedly toward the Inn, entirely unfazed at being a reverse mockery of the old joke about Scotsmen and their kilts.

Ele and Boone stood in a strained silence deeper than the fog. She wanted to apologize for last night, but the right words eluded her. Boone seemed to sense her reticence and started walking.

"Boone, listen…" Ele clutched the sides of her head, fingers tangling in her sleep-raveled hair. "I'm sorry about last night. I shouldn't have…"

Boone bent a little to catch her eyes with his. "It's okay, really."

"No, I was wrong to put you in that position. I don't want you to get the wrong idea, that I just want to sleep with you. I mean, I do… but, I mean…oh, crap. What I'm trying to say is, I was desperate. Wait, no!"

Ele threw her hands up as if to snatch her words from the air. Why did she say that? Again she grabbed both sides of her head and let out a big sigh. "Dammit! Why can't I just say what I want to say?"

She stopped for breath and nervously glanced into Boone's dusky eyes. He was smiling again. Well, that did it. Now she'd never be able to say what she wanted to say.

Oh, to hell with it, Ele thought. She threw her arms around Boone's neck and kissed him, hard. At first it was terrible. Their teeth clacked and their lips met part-mouth, part cheek. No one seemed to know where to put noses and arms, and their bodies bumped at ridiculous angles.

But finally they were kissing, and Ele molded her body to Boone's, relaxing as he drew her into an embrace. She marveled at his chest pressing her breasts, his hips sharp in her belly, his muscular legs warm on her thighs, and his boots crushing the wet grass near her toes.

Then Boone grasped her hair and gently tugged her lips from his. His eyes roamed every line and detail of her features. She wondered, was he looking at her face or penetrating straight into her deepest heart? She studied his face too, and found such kindness, bare desire, love. Love? She ached for him, like no one else, ever.

He continued gazing at Ele, clutching her face, caressing her hair. His bleary black eyes closed as he leaned in for another hungry kiss. Ele responded eagerly, her lips full and reaching – then she retched and the remainder of last night's supper hit the side of Boone's face, thanks to a reflexive head-turn on his part.

Ele leapt back, her eyes widening into blue pools of horror. Boone shook his head and wiped his face with a flannel shirt-sleeve. He looked Ele over once, head to bare feet, and turned on his heel. She watched him walk away into the last wisps of the murky fog.

Ele threw herself into packing the Inn. It had been three days since that foggy morning but she relived it every waking second. She was a raging river of emotions: embarrassed, to say the least, and confused, but mostly she was livid. Was Boone so shallow that an incident like that would change his mind about her? That just couldn't be true. Not the Boone she'd come to trust this much in less than a week. But did she trust him enough to tell him the truth? No, definitely not. If he didn't want her without knowing, she didn't want the pity he would surely extend once he knew.

She shoved more books into a box and violently taped it shut. Uncle Hoyt had given her free rein to pack and sell whatever she wanted. "It's not like I'll remember what I have anyway," he'd quipped, and they both chuckled at his morbid humor. Her uncle had wandered twice in the past three days, but Peachy brought him home mostly dressed each time.

Ele stood and wearily stretched. She adjusted her head kerchief and wiped dirty sweat with the back of her hand, announcing, "Well, that's enough spiders and dust mites for a while."

She left the house and found Uncle Hoyt reclining on a weathered Adirondack chair in the back yard, sipping moonshine and daydreaming. Ele rested one hand on the chair back and ruffled her uncle's hair with the other one.

Unexpectedly, Hoyt spoke of his dementia. "From a medical standpoint, this experience is bizarre. I lose hours in a day, but then clearly remember whole days from way back. I am probably the only person who actually remembers Woodstock. That's where I met Estus, you know."

"Really?" Ele exclaimed, unable to hide her shock. "You went to Woodstock? I never heard this story!" She giggled, flopped down in the grass beside the Adirondack, and crossed her legs at the ankles.

Uncle Hoyt continued, "Yep, I went to Woodstock. For me – well, for a lot of us – it was about trying to fight the Man, end the war, combat the racism. But when I met your aunt, I was just trying to find a dry spot to sit, which was hopeless. I remember Country Joe and the Fish had just finished their set. I came around this van and there was the most beautiful woman I'd ever seen, crouched on the ground, peeing. It was love. I saw stars and hearts.

"Estus was from Savannah, Georgia, and Woodstock for her meant rebelling against her snobbish parents and their old money. Here we were, two exhausted, muddy teenage Southerners, meeting all the way up in New York. I ended up liking her parents very much. And the thing is, Estus' inheritance bought this old place. Ironic, huh?" Her uncle smiled, once again far away in a muddy field, falling in love.

Ele cried, "Oh, Uncle Hoyt, I am so messed up. I ruined everything with Boone."

"Is that so? I think you're being a little hard on yourself. It was just vomit, after all."

"But you weren't there. It was like a chicken soup fountain. Blechhhhhh! What would you have done? I'll tell you, you'd have run, that's what."

"Ele."

"So stupid. I don't blame Boone for stomping off when it happened, but I am upset he hasn't come back. He didn't give me a chance to explain."

"Explain what? People throw up. Animals throw up. Throwing up is a fact of life. Well, unless you're a rat."

"But Boone didn't come back, Uncle Hoyt. He didn't come back and I don't think he will. I'm stupid to think he would. And I'm stupid because I don't have time for a man now anyway. Stupid, stupid, stupid." She dropped her face into her hands and groaned dramatically.

Uncle Hoyt set his glass on the chair arm and leaned forward to look down in Ele's face. "If you think that's who Boone is, then you don't know Boone at all."

He stood and she took his outstretched hand. He hugged her shoulder and said, "There's someone I really think you should talk to." He led her to the river road and Ele realized they were walking to Boone's house.

"Oh, no, Uncle Hoyt. I can't see him, not yet. Please don't." She began to pull away.

"It's not Boone we're seeing."

Ele reluctantly relented, and they walked in silence until they had reached the Buchanan place. He led her up the steps and knocked on the screen door. "Bura, you home?" A voice called back in the affirmative and Hoyt held the screen door open for Ele.

Ele looked around the living room. Despite the house's age and state of unfinished repair, it was tidy and well-ordered. The shelves were festooned with delicate vintage china and figurines, the floor was well swept, and the whole place had been recently dusted. From the kitchen wafted the aroma of freshly-baked goods, and a radio played light country music.

"Ya'll just sit down anywheres," Bura called over the sudsy din of washing dishes. "You want some coffee? I just put a pot on, so it'll be a minute."

Hoyt answered politely, "That would be great, Bura."

In a moment Bura shuffled into the living room with a tray and set it on the coffee table. She adjusted herself down into a love seat that was a newer twin of the one on the porch. "Now what's a-got ya'll out today? Boys ain't a-botherin' you, are they? Let me know if'n they are."

"No, Bura," Hoyt replied, "we're here about Boone."

"Well, I knowed it might be somethin' like that. Girl, I figured he'd be done with all that once you was actually here'n all."

"What do you mean?" Ele said and scooted up on the edge of her chair.

Bura looked over at Hoyt. "You ain't told her nothin'? Well, Law, Law. Call the Confederick law."

Hoyt cleared his throat. "Well, I was meaning to, I just...didn't know how. They hit it off immediately so I thought things would naturally come to light."

"Natrally," replied Bura.

"Can somebody please tell me what is going on?" Ele cried. "Uncle Hoyt, why did you bring me here?"

Hoyt shifted to face her. "There are some things you need to know about Boone, and I think Bura here can best tell you."

Ele frowned nervously at Bura. "What about Boone?"

Bura took a sip of her coffee. "Ahh, well I guess the best place to start is at the beginnin'." With that she set the cup down and motioned for Ele to sit back. "I'm gonna tell you somethin' only family knows. Word of it ain't never left we'uns, ever. Hoyt knows it 'cause he's patched my boys and tended our animals so he's family. You are too, you just don't know it. But you will after I tell you what I'm fixin' to tell you. You listen here, now, and don't int'rupt. Now...where to start?" Her eyes glazed a bit and she began to tell.

CHAPTER 7

"What did you call it, Hoyt?" – Bura

"Boone ain't like you and me. Boone ain't like his brothers or his pa. Boone ain't like nobody 'cept Boone. I found Boone by the river one day. He weren't more than a day old. He was wrapped in a downy quilt and was in a plastic laundry basket. To this day I don't know where he come from. We had this big ol' rain the night before and I was just a-wanderin' around seein' what had washed up. Well, there he was and you know, despite all that rain, he was dry as a corn-crib. He wasn't cryin' or nothin,' just a-layin' there all tucked in like someone knowed I was comin.' I looked all up and down the river that day but I could'n find hide or hair of anybody. You see, I had just lost a baby about a week afore; it were a britches baby. I figured God had done wanted to correct things so He sent me my little baby boy, just like Moses from the Bible. So I named him Moses 'cause I figured that was what God wanted. His pa said we oughta name him Boone, 'cause it'd be a boon to have another boy around to help with chores and such. I won out for a while, but we'll get to that later.

"No one in town questioned the baby as mine, seein' as I had my other two at home and how I never told no one I lost the other one. Doc Henry suspected but he never said anythin' that I know of. Things went on as normal. The other boys doted on him and helped me out. Anse – well, Anse is Anse. But even he took to Moses like nothin' else. I cain't tell you what it was. It was like if'n you looked in his eyes, somethin' changed about you. You could be in the illest mood, but his eyes and smile just melted you and you felt like things were going to be okay. He was the gentlest, quietest baby I ever knowed. Never cried, not once except if'n he was hungry or wet. When he got older I'd catch him just a-sittin', playin' with the dust in a sunbeam gigglin' to himself. At first I thought I had got me another simple one like Squirrel but it weren't like that. He would look at you and then back to the sunbeam like you should be a-seein' what he was seein.'

"By the time he could walk and talk, we really knowed he was diff'rent. He knowed and remembered things a baby should'n know. He talked real early and walked real early. The real shocker for us'ns was when I'd read to him of a-night, he'd be real intent on what was being said. He'd point out if'n you skipped a word or a page. Soon he was askin' for more books. I knowed a lady at the li-bary who'd bring me books they was throwin' out. Moses read them as fast as I could bring 'em to him.

"Now I know some folks don't think that's too particular. I did'n neither at the time. See, Arbuckle had his gift too, pickin' up mechanic'n early, and Squirrel was always a fair hand to bird callin' and wood carvin' and such.   "But Moses was different. Most kids'll look at the same book over and over and get a kick out of it ever' time like it was brand new. Not Moses. Once he read a book, he did'n pick it up again and always asked for a different one.

"Now, I tell you, I'm ashamed my boys did'n get much schoolin.'

Their Pa 'needed' them all to work. I tried my best to get him to at least let Moses go. I argued he was too smart to be doin' 'shine or labor work. Anse would holler back that hard work was more important than some ol' useless book learnin'. Hard work, hunh. Anse would'n know a hard day's work if'n it bit him. Only time he works hard is when he's huntin' and fishin.' But I tell you what I done. I slipped that boy a new book ever' chance I got. I was'n about to let his noggin go to waste. But I still wish I woulda snuck him off to school somehow.

"When Moses was about six was when we discovered what made him so different. What did you call it, Hoyt? I-dactic memory or some such jargon."

"Eidetic," Hoyt corrected, motioning for Bura to continue.

"But it's much more than that, I tell you. It ain't just that he remembers words on a page or some such. He really remembers things. If'n it happens to him, he cain't never forget it. You ask him anythin' about somethin' he done, he can tell you what was said word-for-word, moment-to-moment. He'll tell you what you were wearin', what ya'll ate, what everthin' smelled like, you name it.

"Now here's the sad thing though. If'n it was a sad day, he remembers it too. He'll bawl like a baby calf if'n it was real bad, just like it was happenin' right there and then. Sometimes I wonder if'n he remembers his first ma.

"When he was about six or so, he could tell you I'm sure, you and your ma started comin' to the Inn regular in the summer. That boy did'n know what to do. There had been other young'uns that had come to the Inn but he never seemed int'rested in a-playin' with them. Somethin' about you though. I did'n see it. There had been prettier and friendlier girls that had come, but you was somethin' special to him. Why ever' single evenin' he'd come runnin' in here a-tellin' me what Ele and him had done that day. Law have mercy I like to never got him to shut up and go to sleep. Anse did'n mind though, 'cause that boy'd hop outta' bed and hit his chores and then tear up the road to the Inn to be with you.

"Then one day he come in with his side stitched up and a big grin on his face. He declared that from now on he did'n want to talk country anymore 'cause he wanted to be 'sphisticated' like the city boys where Ele lived. He also told us he wanted to be called Boone 'cause Ele said Moses was an old man's name. So we had to call him Boone from then on. He would'n answer to nothin' else. I believe the boy woulda starved if'n I had called him Moses to come to supper.

"Then the summer he was nine, he came in a-grinnin' and declarin' he was gettin' married. I said, 'You are? To who?' I'll never forget the look on his face when he said, 'To Ele, of course. We are to be wed when we are old enough. We can't now because we're only nine.' I laughed and hurt his feelin's a little. Then you and your ma left that fall and never came back, so I figured that was that.

"Boone never forgot though, never. The local girls all came 'round a-gigglin' and whatnot tryin' to get him to notice. He never fell in with 'em. He never went out with his brothers neither, when they'd go carousin' and the like. He said he made a promise to Elenora and he was waitin' on her. Said it would'n be proper for Ele to be with a man who did those kinda things.

"Ever' year Boone waited for summer and ever' year I'd see him a-walkin' back home with that hang-dog look. And sometimes he'd just cry and cry, and I'd hold him. Ain't nobody cries like that for someone unless they's love in it.

"Law, when he was barely growed he took all his savin's from his odd jobs and bought us this little place so he could be right down the pasture from 'Ele's house,' he called it. Then he put a lamp in the window ever' night just in case you came back and saw it.

"Elenora, that boy loves you. And it goes beyond anythin' we can know. It's like a force of nature, like the wind or the river out there. You can put up a wall or a dam and stop it for awhile, but eventually, it'll bust on through and get where it wants to go. You cain't stop it, no ma'am, no way."

CHAPTER

8

"Are you going anywhere in particular?" – Boone

Ele spent the rest of the day in pensive thought. That evening after she made sure Uncle Hoyt was safely in bed, she wandered out on the porch. She hugged her arms, peered down at the river, and let her eyes wander, not for the first time, to the distant light at the end of the pasture. The light meant Boone, and Ele realized Boone was still burning it for her, which made his current behavior that much more bewildering. If he loved her so much, why the rejection, why the distance?

She scratched the back of her head and trailed her long pale curls through her fingers. Why was she even allowing herself to have feelings for him? Wasn't it foolish to let him in? Of course it was. She shouldn't – no, couldn't – afford to care about Boone. Despite what he felt, what she felt, there could be no "them." Especially if what Bura said was true, that Boone had never touched another woman because he was waiting for her! In light of that, her past was definitely too shameful, her current situation even worse.

So her rejection would hurt, for sure, and he would remember it forever, but at least he would remember an Ele that was still somewhat closer to the crystalline one he wanted and deserved – instead of the one his broken heart would remember if she told him her past, her secrets. So she just wouldn't tell him.

She hitched a hip on the porch railing and stared down at the silvery-mooned river, its relentless, hypnotic song reminding her of Bura's words about the elemental power of Boone Buchanan. She could stand in the dusk and feel his strength, wrapped in a soft blanket of gentleness, as if he were against the rail next to her.

Okay, so if she was being honest, at least part of the reason she didn't want him to learn her secrets was she just knew he would think less of her, most likely reject her, and then she could add heartbreak to the problems she already faced.

No, it was better to leave Boone alone, throw herself into the house and her uncle; then, afterward, she could pack her secrets away and carry them back to New York among relative strangers. Then when Boone learned the truth – it's not like she could hide it – she wouldn't be here to face him.

A katydid landed on the rail beside her. It pirouetted and ambled up to her thigh. She reached down and delicately picked it up, remembering what Uncle Hoyt had said about katydids. "Hear that, Ele? Ninety days after the katydid's song until the first killing frost." The sound always made her sad, for it meant soon her mother and she would be leaving.

She tried to resist looking again at the distant golden light, but failed. She did love him, but she had to leave. She tossed the insect into the air and watched as it winged off into the moonlight toward the river.

The next morning there was no naked uncle playing bagpipes

or butchering chickens. Uncle Hoyt was gone from his room, so Ele presumed he'd headed into town again. She worried less now, knowing the townsfolk were watching over him, especially Peachy. She stood at the threshold of the room she had been packing up the night before, and blew out a big huff. She had not experienced any nausea this morning and was actually ravenous. Just then biscuits and gravy sounded good, though she had not had any since she was a little girl. And she knew just where to get them.

She snatched up her keys and drove into town, expecting any moment to see her uncle and Peachy returning with coffee. But they weren't along the road, and soon she pulled into a diagonal space in front of the Town Square Cafe. There was no sign of any Buchanans, Boone or otherwise, much to her relief. She pushed the door open and found a booth by the window.

A new waitress, not Del, took her order and poured her a cup of scalding black coffee. She blew across the steaming liquid, barely hearing the ambient conversation as she pondered idly if Del had had her twins yet. The window afforded a decent view of the square, where preparations were underway for some upcoming event. When the waitress returned, Ele inquired about it.

"Oh, that's for the Canning Festival this weekend. You should come, it's always a bunch of fun," she told Ele.

Ele thanked her and began to dig into the sinfully delicious breakfast. She was grateful to have skipped the nausea this morning because her vomit often resembled the food she was currently enjoying. She ate with gusto and found herself in such better spirits that she wished there was a biscuit-and-gravy cure for everything.

She sopped the last pool of gravy with a biscuit corner as she once again looked outside. Her heart simultaneously jumped and sank. Across the square, Boone and his brothers were piling out of his truck. With them was an older, lanky man Ele assumed was Anse, their father. The elder man hobbled out on the grass and peered around intently, his arms gesturing in grand Biblical motions. The sons fell to the work, whereas Anse limped over to the nearest shaded bench and settled on it like a throne.

Ele's eyes inevitably drifted to Boone. In spite of her twisted emotions, she couldn't deny he was so very handsome. She watched him move with calculated grace. In fact, all three sons worked with one accord, economical and precise, under Anse's scowling command. Twenty minutes later the king and his subjects had erected several booths, and Arby and Squirrel turned their attention to stringing lights while Boone strode off toward the main stage erected on the square's opposite corner.

Suddenly Ele realized how long she had occupied the booth while leaning on her hand and mooning at the Buchanans. Slightly flustered, ignoring the waitress's amused expression, she tossed a ten on the table and exited. Hands in her jean pockets, she crossed the street into the square and glanced down the way Boone had gone, but didn't spot him.

Then he was there, standing next to her. She felt his presence long before she looked his way. He just stood there, saying nothing, so she broke the awkward silence.

"Um, yeah, so how's all the building and setting-up going?"

"We're at a standstill," Boone replied. "A load of lumber coming in from Asheville was supposed to be here by now. Can't do much until it does. Are you going anywhere in particular? Can I walk you?"

"Uh, sure. I was just headed up to the..um...real estate office." She hoped he hadn't noticed the pause as she constructed the lie. But of course he noticed, she thought. His mother said he noticed and remembered everything.

He walked apart from her along the curb, giving room to let the elephant between them walk as well. She sensed he wanted to talk about the other morning, but she didn't know how to begin. Any words she did try to say entwined like honeysuckle behind her lips.

And his eyes on her were no help either. She glanced up and caught him looking, and he immediately turned to feint interest in a shop window display.

"Look," she spouted finally, "I'm sorry for the other morning. I don't know what happened, I guess I was just nervous or had a… stomach thing or whatever."

"Ele…"

"No, don't interrupt. I've got to talk before I lose my mind. I don't know what you think of me. I don't honestly know for sure how I feel about you." Well, she thought, that was certainly a lie, but she was in this now. It was time to push him away for good.

Boone motioned for her to sit on a nearby bench. Ele continued without pause, "The thing is – I like you, Boone. But..."

His eyes scanned hers. "Ele, just speak. I'm here. I'm not going anywhere."

She looked at the pavement. Yeah, but you will, she thought. "You are wonderful, but I'm a mess. You don't know what kind of a screwed-up lump of crap you'd get with me." She fixed her eyes on the ground, knowing if she made eye contact she might bawl like a baby.

"Ele, please look at me," Boone pleaded, but Ele kept her eyes down. "Forget all the feelings and 'like' stuff and just talk to me. Forget I'm Boone. Think of me as just a friend – or your Uncle Hoyt. Just two friends, one talking, the other listening. That's all."

She stared at her hands for a moment, trying to piece the words together. "Boone, I know you want me. I know you have…deep feelings for me. But I can't love you back. I just can't."

"I understand," Boone responded.

"You do? How?" Ele exclaimed, finally looking up at him.

"You're involved with someone already." He nodded his head.

"What? No!" she protested.

"It's okay, Ele. I know about Mike. I accidentally overheard you leaving that voicemail the other day. I know you two are making plans, and I won't get in the way if that's what you want. I just wanted a chance to let you know how I feel. How I've always felt.

"I love you, Ele. Have since I was six years old. I always will. But I wouldn't do anything to hurt you, and that includes getting in the way of your wedding if you really love Mike."

"Wedding? No, it's not like that. I mean, sure, Mike and I were together for a bit, but it's been over for awhile. He's a good friend, but we are not getting married," she stated emphatically, shaking her head. "Mike is definitely not marrying me."

"But he should. If this Mike were an honorable man, he would. I would! There's no way I would let you have my baby and not take care of both of you. Nothing would make me happier than to have a family with you." Hands clenching into stout fists, Boone's jaw tightened and his countenance clouded. "Maybe I'll take a trip to New York and set Mike straight," he threatened.

"Whatever in the world are you talking about?" Ele cried. "Why would you do that? Family? Baby? Boone, I'm not pregnant!" She stared at Boone in bald shock.

His face lost color and he stammered, "But, I thought... you said you were throwing up in the morning and you talked about plans and churches and flowers with Mike...I just assumed..."

The absurdity of the situation suddenly clear, Ele's eyes crinkled and she snorted. Then, like a bursting dam, she howled with laughter. Attempting to catch her breath in the midst of unrestrained guffaws, Ele rubbed her face and wiped her eyes. She managed to squeak, "You...thought..." and the giggles began anew. The mirth became so much she nearly rolled off the bench. "That's why you walked away... you thought..."

Boone, bewildered and irritated, hid behind his hand in embarrassment. But soon he found her laughter contagious and grinned a little himself.

Ele "hoo-hooed" until she could get her breath again. "Oh, wow," she exclaimed, "I haven't laughed like that in a long while." Somewhat composed, she took Boone's hands and gazed into those exquisite black eyes. "Look, there is nothing going on between Mike and me. And I am certainly not pregnant."

Boone tilted his head in confusion. Ele suddenly realized she either had to explain or forever hold her peace, and her silly mood instantly evaporated like water in a hot cast-iron skillet. Despite her firm decision to keep the truth from Boone, she found the words rising unchecked from her throat. "You see, Boone," Ele began, fluttering heartbeat thrumming in her neck, "Mike is – "

It was at that very moment Ele realized she had been hearing for some time the incessant bark of a distant dog. Now the frantic barking grew much closer, accompanied by a strange mechanical grinding.

"What in the..." Ele gasped. She and Boone turned together at the sound and could see Peachy running full-tilt just behind a flatbed truck full of lumber thundering down the hill toward them. The driver-less truck swerved and caromed off cars parked along the street, crumpling and smashing everything in its path. Boone swept up Ele and dashed across the grass barely in time to avoid being struck. Just beyond at the far side of the square, perched on their usual bench, the War Brides moved with amazing alacrity for women of their advanced age.

Ele saw the next events with slow, crystal clarity. Coming up the sidewalk, having just left the cafe and crossed the street, was Uncle Hoyt. His exit could not have been more ill-timed. Looking up to see the rolling monster approaching, he dropped his coffee and froze.

Ele screamed. Boone shoved her aside and sprinted behind the truck in an attempt to save her uncle, but Ele's insides turned to water because it was clear Boone wouldn't make it.

Then a furry blur flew past Ele and darted just in front of the metal beast. Ele saw Hoyt go down hard on the pavement as Peachy barreled into him and took his place before the full brunt of the vehicle's overpowering force. The truck slammed into Peachy, glanced off the trunk of a maple tree, and hopped over several parked cars, finally, finally coming to a stop. The impact threw Peachy across the street and through the plate-glass cafe window, taking curtains and blinds with him.

Terrified shock paralyzed Ele for several seconds before she noticed her uncle slumped against the base of the tree. Then adrenaline surged and she dashed down across the lawn. Boone was there first, checking Hoyt over while her uncle insisted he was unhurt. Ele embraced him in a fierce hug, "Uncle Hoyt!"

She was still hugging her uncle when she noticed Boone walking slowly toward the truck and the cafe. She put her hand to her mouth. "Oh, Peachy. Oh, no."

Hoyt stood and made his way around the truck. Lumber strewn about the streets made navigation difficult, and Boone was already inside the cafe before Hoyt and Ele managed to reach the door. Inside, Peachy lay calm and quiet in a pool of blood, glass, and blinds. Only an occasional raspy breath betrayed his distress. Boone knelt beside him and began gingerly clearing debris. He then stroked the devastated animal's head, whispering comfort.

Hoyt knelt beside Boone, ignoring the sharp shards of plate glass, and expertly palpated the dog's broken and bloody head, neck, body, legs. He looked at Boone and shook his head. "It'll only be another minute or two. I don't have anything to give him, but it won't be long. Just keep soothing him."

Ele cried with the terror of nearly losing her uncle, the wrenching sight of Peachy's horrible suffering, and the heartbreak of watching her beloved Boone hold precious Peachy during his last breaths.

Boone cradled Peachy's head until, with a slight shudder and groan, Peachy passed. Boone pressed his face into the dog's fur and wailed in anguish. Ele sobbed harder when she realized that this event, every horrific and graphic second, would be forever etched in Boone's memory.

Hoyt stood and placed his hands on Boone's head. He motioned for Ele to take his place at Boone's side, and she helped Boone stand and embraced him. He let out a long sigh and nodded, pushing the grief aside momentarily to do what now had to be done.

Arbuckle and Squirrel arrived and laid a paint tarp down beside the still form. Squirrel carefully wrapped the dog, and Boone grasped Ele's hand for support as Arbuckle carried Peachy's body from the cafe to the bed of Boone's truck. As the boys left, Uncle Hoyt instructed them to take Peachy to the Inn so he could clean him up. Boone and Ele followed them out into the sunshine.

Fire-engine sirens whined through the air, and the Wayah police were busy questioning any witnesses and the truck driver, who had apparently stepped into a store to ask directions when the truck popped out of gear.

Boone did not let go of Ele's hand as they listened to the details. "I'll be a-stayin' here to help clean up," he said, grief bringing out his mountain dialect. "Take Hoyt home and I'll be on directly."

"Okay," Ele replied, still shaking. She hated to leave, but knew he had to deal with this on his own.

Hoyt hugged Boone and patted his back. "He saved me, son. Now you take that as it is meant to be. He saved me. Don't let all this," he waved his hand around at the carnage, "be how you remember Peachy. Remember him with love. Who Peachy was, and how you love him – well, you've got to screw that to the sticking place of a mind you have. He is a hero." They both stood a moment before Hoyt gave Boone's shoulder a final squeeze. "See you at the house, son."

Ele's eyes met Boone's. With a sharp intake of breath and a small smile, he walked across the square and joined his brothers at the truck.

67

CHAPTER 9

"Do you love Boone?" - Uncle Hoyt

The next day was overcast with leaden clouds, reflecting the town's mood. The crowd on the square was somber, speaking only occasionally in reverent tones. Hoyt walked with his arm around Ele, and soon they were at Boone's side. Ele looked at the gathered crowd; most of the faces were familiar and she guessed nearly everyone in the town was present. Adjacent to the Grady Shelton statue several chairs and benches had been set up. A bright garland of flowers circled a fresh plot of dirt next to the statue's pedestal, about six feet from the improvised seating. Bura was among the front-row attendees, and Arbuckle and Anse stood behind her chair.

Ele was wondering where Squirrel was when Pastor Grant stepped forward and shushed the murmuring crowd. He spoke proudly and kindly of Peachy, emphasizing he had never before eulogized a dog. "I think we all agree, however, that Peachy was more than a dog. He was our friend. Our companion. Our guardian," he looked over at

Hoyt, "and our hero. Though he was a dog, he exemplified the best of our town and community. He will be missed, and he will never be replaced in our hearts. Let us pray."

Ele shuddered a cry. She felt a hand in hers and Boone stood beside her. The prayer ended, and Hoyt stepped forward, producing Peachy's leash from his pocket and laying it on the mound of flowers. He stepped back, wiping an eye.

From behind Ele, a high-lonesome voice began singing. Not wanting to call attention to herself, she listened without looking back. The song was unfamiliar, and the lyrics captivated her.

In these trials of life I find
Another voice inside my mind
He comforts me and bids me live
Inside the love the Father gives.

Ele had never heard a voice quite like this. Finally, curiosity overrode decorum, and she risked a glance to see the singer. He was obscured by the crowd for a moment and she moved her head around to no avail. Boone noticed her efforts and gently pulled her a step back for a clear view. When she saw the singer, she had to make a conscious effort to close her shocked mouth. That trembling, heart-rending voice emanated from none other than Squirrel Buchanan.

His eyes were cast skyward, arms raised with hands reaching to Heaven. Holy power flowed through his voice and Ele found herself transfixed as Squirrel's song, like clean snowfall, blanketed the mourning townsfolk. Many were closing their eyes and swaying in peaceful joy. Ele too was taken by the moment and felt her heart soar. She looked at Boone, who was nodding proudly.

The song ended much too soon, and Squirrel lowered his hands and head, his face reverting to the childlike simplicity Ele had come to know. She caught his eye and smiled. He immediately looked away, but just as quickly turned to her and flashed his boyish grin.

The crowd dispersed as people returned to their vehicles and stores. The solemn gray mood seemed to lift in spite of the sky's continued oppression. Soon the volume of conversation rose and festival set-up proceeded.

"I've got to change and finish working on the cafe and setting up for the evening's music," Boone said. "Can I pick you up tonight?"

"No," Ele replied, "Uncle Hoyt is riding with me. Plus, I need to buy something in Asheville this afternoon. So get to work, and I'll see you later."

She walked back to her uncle, still standing by the little flower-festooned grave. She took his arm and they walked to the Subaru. Boone waved, heading under the completed pavilion just as the first spatterings of rain began.

In spite of the downpour, Ele made the trip to Asheville and back in under three hours. She found a dress and shoes to match in one store, a feat impossible in New York. The drive provided considerable time to ponder the past two days' events. And the decision she had made last night.

Before yesterday's tragedy, Ele was prepared to break Boone's heart and take the consequences with her to New York. But Peachy's heroism and Uncle Hoyt's brush with death forced her to ask hard questions and face indisputable answers.

In just a handful of days Ele had glimpsed the surface of Boone's character, but didn't fathom its depth until yesterday. Peachy's sacrifice to save her uncle had in no way superseded the significance of Boone's herculean dash to reach him. She knew full well: had Boone not saved her first, he would have taken Peachy's position. Such self-sacrifice, such reckless love, she had craved since her mother died – yet never found it until now.

Boone loved Ele, and she loved Boone! But acting on that love was plunging recklessly into murky and dangerous waters – that she knew. Nevertheless, it was settled in her mind: she would confess her feelings and fully embrace the joy of their love, opening the floodgates to an elemental force too long dammed. She was meant for Boone Buchanan, and he for her. They would love tonight, and tomorrow she would tell him everything. Oh, then the hurt to come. But he had proven, she believed with every broken cell in her being, he would accept her no matter what polluted past, present, and future monster reared its head.

Pulling up to the Inn, Ele was overpowered by rolling nausea accompanied by a stabbing headache behind her eye. Apparently her musings, coupled with the twisted road and steady rain, had wrecked her constitution. Her uncle ordered her to lie down for a bit, assuring her the real fun didn't happen until later. Too ill to protest, Ele conceded and fell into a deep sleep.

Upon awakening, she panicked. The room was as dark as the outside sky. She checked her phone and saw with relief it was only five pm. The nap had staved off the edge of her headache and nausea, and she made a mental note to thank her uncle for insisting upon it. She arose and walked to the window.

The rain was heavy and accompanied by gusty wind. She looked toward Boone's house for the comforting light, then realized the family would already be at the Festival.

She showered, dressed, and examined herself in the mirror. The scarlet dress poured over her curves like red wine. She could barely wait to savor Boone's reaction when he saw her. She applied her makeup sparingly, to contrast the dress; too much and she would look like a hooker. She could just hear Bura's "Law, Law! Call the Confederick law!"   Downstairs she found Uncle Hoyt working a crossword in his recliner. She was glad to see he was fully clothed. "What do you think?" She twirled. "Too much?"

"Whoa!' Uncle Hoyt cried, then whistled in admiration. "Hot

mama! I think you're going to blind the boy. You realize the young women in this town already hate you for taking Boone. Now you've gone and outright declared war and dropped an atom bomb with the first salvo."

"You think it's too much? I'll change."

"Nonsense! You could dress in a tater sack and it would make little difference to Boone. Boy, I wish your aunt and Joy could see you. You look like your ma. She'd be so proud of you. I'm proud of you."

"Thanks, Uncle Hoyt. I know you say that because you have to, but it makes me feel good anyway."

He stood abruptly, tossing the newspaper to the floor. "Now, you listen here, Elenora Estus Reese," he declared. "I have never lied to you, so what I am telling you now is the truth. You are a beautiful, wonderful girl and nothing does my heart better than to see you and Boone together."

"I'm sorry, Uncle Hoyt. It's just hard sometimes to accept love, especially when you know you don't deserve it."

"Do you love Boone?" Her uncle took her by the shoulders and looked her in the eye.

"Yes."

"Then tell him the truth, Ele. Don't keep things from him."

"What do you mean?" she demanded. Then, in that moment, in her uncle's face, she saw it.

He knew.

"You know, don't you? How long have you known?"

"Mike Wojcik called me a couple of weeks ago when he learned you were coming here. Now, listen, don't get mad at him. He wasn't trying to be unethical; he just needed someone he could trust to watch out for you."

"Still, he had no right!" Ele backed up a step, trembling with indignation. "That wasn't for him to tell. I didn't want you to know. I didn't want to worry you!"

"Oh, shut up, you. I may be just a veterinarian with dementia, but I would have figured it out and asked questions anyway."

Ele crossed her arms and sorted through a boiling mass of emotions. She wasn't too surprised to discover that she felt mostly relief. "You're right, Uncle Hoyt. I'm sorry. And I am going to tell him – tomorrow. I just want tonight to be perfect."

Uncle Hoyt nodded and placed his hands on her shoulders again. "Go back upstairs and fix your makeup. I'll go put on some dancin' and drinkin' clothes. Then let's go party."

CHAPTER 10

"But aren't they afraid of the law?" – Ele

Parking was at a premium and she and Uncle Hoyt had to walk several streets in the downpour. They shared an immense golf umbrella but the wind whipped wet spray under and around them. Ele was fairly drenched, the overcoat she wore having offered little protection. The dress was already sexy, skimming every curve, with its deep v-shaped neckline framing a valley of cleavage while the short flouncy skirt exposed an expanse of thigh. Now, soaking wet, the dress approached obscene. She pulled the coat snugly around her and stepped with her uncle through the pavilion's opening.

Inside, the atmosphere was bright, raucous, and convivial, in direct contrast to the day's sorrow and nasty weather. Couples and groups were laughing, eating, and dancing to the fiery bluegrass band featuring Arbuckle on guitar and Squirrel on banjo. Already enthralled by Squirrel's magic voice, Ele was pleased to hear Arbuckle crooning pretty well too.

Boone found Ele almost immediately. Realizing she was soaked, he brought her to a table close to the outdoor heaters the town had set up to combat the chilly damp. She stripped off the sopping coat and waited for Boone's reaction. Looking up from draping the coat on a chair, Boone cleared his throat while his eyes lingered on her body.

"Eyes up here, cowboy, eyes up here. Maybe later if you're real good I might let you have a dance."

He stammered, "Might?"

"Well, I'm sure there will be prospects before the night is through. I paid a lot for this dress, so I plan to get a few free drinks out of it."

Boone grinned and turned beet red. In that small moment any fear, doubt, and loneliness disappeared. Ele truly loved him. If this was her only night of happiness with him, wasn't that worth it? She took his hand, and he happily thread his fingers between hers.

Settling under the heater to warm up, Ele scanned the room for familiar faces in the crowd. Anse and Bura were seated across the dance floor, each engaged in conversation with other townsfolk. Ele noticed Anse regularly reach across and grasp Bura's hand, a simple loving gesture that struck her as out of place for a man of Anse's gruff demeanor. Not far from them was Uncle Hoyt sitting with three very attractive women, all easily ten years his junior. Each of them would occasionally touch his arm or hand as they laughed at his antics.

The music set stopped, the applause amplified by the rain on the pavilion's metal roof and canvas sides. Arbuckle and Squirrel, instead of sitting with their parents or even Ele and Boone, slipped to a corner table and began dispersing small jars of clear liquid. A short conversation with the customer, a discreet exchange of money and beverage, and on to the next table.

"Boone, isn't that liquor your brothers are peddling?"

"Yep."

"Well…isn't that, you know…illegal?"

"Sure."

"What if they get caught?"

"Ele, this is called the Cannin' Festival, but truth be told, it should be called the Buchanan Festival." Ele giggled at the pun as Boone explained. "Everyone here comes for the liquor. Oh sure, there are pies and okra and corn and stuff, but that's in the daytime. The real event happens in the evening."

"But aren't they afraid of the law?"

"Well, let me put it this way: the guy there at that table is Judge Allen. The man he's playing cards with is a former ABC officer. Alcoholic Beverage Control," he elaborated at Ele's quizzical expression. "Uh, let's see… the guy playing the upright bass is a deputy, and the man who's just now carrying out a case – see, over there? – is the sheriff. So I don't think it's much of a problem."

"I see."

"Yeah, the Buchanans have been making corn liquor since the Civil War. Arbuckle has perfected the formula beyond all science. I'm pretty sure he uses magic."

"Do you drink it?"

"Actually, no. It's funny isn't it? I don't like being out of control. Besides, who would drive everyone home later?"

She looked again at Bura and Anse. "What's the deal with your parents? Do they love each other?"

"My father is probably the meanest man on the planet. In fact, I truly believe he makes a point to be so. I know a son shouldn't think of his father that way, but it's the truth. When I say mean, I don't mean cruel. He just has a way, his way, that everything needs to be done. He won't do things himself, mind you, but they have to be done his way.

"Did you know he was a war hero? It's true. Unarmed, he single-handedly fended off an entire company of VC after his patrol was ambushed. I mean single-handedly. The men say he tore off his shirt and waded into them, wailing and flailing like a madman. He was shot three times and stabbed through the hip, hence the limp. I asked him about it once, and all he would say was he did it because he needed to get home to Momma."

"Bura."

"Yeah, believe it or not, my momma used to be one of the most beautiful women in the county. She told me Pa was hellbent on making her his and no man on God's green earth could stop him. I guess he proved it."

"Wow. I never even knew my father," Ele said. "My mom wouldn't talk about him. Honestly, I don't think she was sure who he was. Sometimes that bothered me, but she was such a devoted mother and for awhile I had Uncle Hoyt and Aunt Estus in the summers."

Ele was still looking at Boone's parents. "Your momma and daddy," Ele said, squeezing Boone's hand intertwined with hers on the table. "Do you think that kind of fierce love still exists?"

He squeezed her hand back. "Yes I do."

Arbuckle and crew returned to the stage and began to play a lively bluegrass tune. Boone asked Ele, "Are you dry enough to dance?"

"Absolutely!" Ele cried. "Let's do it!"

Boone pulled Ele to the floor, and they danced as if they had rehearsed for years. After a couple of songs, they switched partners for a reel, but then the boys strummed a slow tune and Boone found Ele and clasped her close to his body. Once in awhile he would brush her lips with his, but the crush of the crowd and his natural modesty kept him from lingering there.

Placing his mouth near her ear as they swayed to the soft guitar, Boone said, "You need to know, Ele, that I will never, ever hurt you. I always keep my promises, Ele. I mean it. I will never let you go. I've waited twenty years to be here with you. I can't stand another moment without you."

Ele stopped dancing and looked straight at him. Wow, those eyes. "What are you saying, Boone?"

"Marry me, Elenora."

She should have been surprised. She wasn't. She should have taken time to consider. She didn't.

"Yes, yes, yes!" Ele cried.

Boone stepped back, clapped his hands, and fairly skipped onto the stage. The band plinked a few more awkward chords, then stopped. Grabbing the microphone from his brother, Boone shouted, "Hey, everybody! Ele and I are getting married!"

The crowd cheered.

"About damn time!" shouted Bura. "Well don't just stand there like an idiot, you fool boy! Kiss her already!"

"If you don't, I will!" exclaimed Arbuckle to a burst of laughter from the crowd.

Boone leapt from the stage, swept Ele into his arms, and hungrily sought her mouth. Only the loud "Whoo-hoos" and whistles of the crowd stopped them, and Boone's face turned red again. The townsfolk surrounded the couple, the men shaking Boone's hand and slapping him on the back, the women weeping joyfully and pulling Ele into long hugs. Over the shoulder of the Italian War Bride, she saw Anse hug Bura, who dabbed her eyes with a paper napkin.

Ele turned to find Uncle Hoyt, but instead saw Gilliam Thrasbick fling the tent flap aside and split the crowd with his slick yellow rain suit and deliberate strides to the stage. He picked up a microphone, clearly distressed as he raised a hand for everyone's attention.

"Folks, I've just come from the reservoir. Lundy says the dam machinery is busted and he can't open the sluices. To make a long story short, she'll go over the top in about two hours, or she may break any moment. If you got kinfolk along the Cane, you best get to 'em and get 'em to high ground in town. Go to the courthouse on this side of the river – or if you get trapped on the other side, go to the high school gym. You need help, give me a holler. I got my radio on and I'll do what I can. Be careful, folks, and God bless."

The crowd dispersed in waves of worried murmurs. Boone led Ele back to the table and helped her slide into her damp coat.

Ele looked around. "Where's Uncle Hoyt? Boone, where's Hoyt?"

Boone slid through clumps of exiting people and began asking questions. Several folks shook their heads.

Then Arbuckle said, "I saw him heading out around the third or fourth song. I was playing. I didn't think nothing of it, brother."

"Oh, Boone," cried Ele, "he could be anywhere!"

Boone calmly responded, "Squirrel, you take care of Momma and Daddy. Arby, you check the streets around here. Ele, take your car down 17W to the ugly bridge. It's on higher ground. I'll take my truck over the hill and down the pasture near my house to look for him on the river road. We'll meet up at the Inn. We'll find him. Or maybe he's already home," Boone said hopefully, but the look on his face betrayed his doubts.

CHAPTER 11

"I believe that's my house you're on." – *Boone*

Ele's fear intensified with every mile she sped down 17W. The rain made visibility very poor, and she almost missed turning onto the ugly bridge. Thumping over its crumbly concrete surface, Ele could hear the ravenous rush of water and feel it pounding against the bridge. "Oh, God, please let him be at home already, please."

Leaves and small branches whipped under the Subaru as it slid and spun up the driveway through the curtain of rain. Despite the downpour, Ele rolled down the windows and turned the lights on high beam, shouting her uncle's name and occasionally blowing the horn. The Inn was completely dark, and when she arrived at the turnout for the footbridge, her heart sank. A lone figure, hunched against the wind, swayed in the middle of the footbridge.

She slammed the car into park and jumped out. The wind had increased considerably, whipping the bridge like a parade banner. Tossing her high heels in the muddy grass, Ele gingerly stepped onto the first plank, clenching the side cables while placing each foot with excruciating deliberation. "Uncle Hoyt, are you okay? Uncle Hoyt!"

He lifted his face, which appeared to melt in the rain. "Ele! Ele! I found you! Your aunt has supper ready!"

Oh, no, thought Ele. "Uncle Hoyt, we have to go! It's not safe!" she shouted.

The Subaru's headlights skipped across the river just to the left of the little bridge, and Ele could clearly see the livid water churning over and over itself. She had never seen it this high. She had never seen any river this high. She figured the water to be only five or six feet below the bridge.

"Uncle Hoyt, you have to come with me." She took a few more tentative steps toward him, her feet splayed wide for balance. Even as she inched closer, he still seemed a mile away. The wind gusted, the rain intensified, and the bridge bucked like a bull determined to dislodge her and Uncle Hoyt both.

Ele fought the urge to scream, terrified it would scare her uncle into going the opposite way. "Just stay there, Uncle Hoyt!" she shouted over the snarling water. "I'm coming, just hang on!" Her feet skidded out and she scrambled to plant them again. Inch by unending inch she moved forward.   Several more times she paused to adjust her grip and footing before moving forward. The steel cabling bit into her palms and blood intermingled with the rain for a more tenuous hold. She finally reached Uncle Hoyt and grasped his shirt, crying, "Are you okay?" She looked in his face and he nodded. "Okay, let's get you home."

There was a profound boom over the water. It wasn't thunder. Ele jerked her head to peer upriver where the headlights flickered. Creaks and snaps accompanied the boom now, and an immense shadowy mass tumbled toward the bridge.

"Oh God, what is that?" Ele shrieked. The mass rushed at them, a writhing mob of stumps and lumber that rose up and then fell on the bridge like a breaching Leviathan. "Don't look, Uncle Hoyt!" screamed Ele, scrambling to cover him. "Don't look!"

The mass exploded around the bridge, spinning its cables and planks around and around like a child's string toy. Ele's body entwined around her uncle between the cables like an insect spun up by a giant spider. She felt her left shin snap, then a grisly pop in her right hip – and then the bridge flung them at the great mass.

Wedged underneath on two enormous boulders were the splintered remains of a house. Ele and Uncle Hoyt sprawled on its roof a few feet below the footbridge which, despite dangling a few stripped cables and missing several planks, remained miraculously attached to its pylons at both ends. Ele, attempting to get her bearings as raindrops stung her eyes, felt the mass shift under her. She knew it would break loose in a matter of moments – and they would be swept away.

"Ele!" Boone's voice rang out over the drumming rain, "Ele! I'm almost to you! Hang on!"

Boone appeared at the bridge's end, silhouetted in the Subaru's headlights. Defying the rocking, swaying bridge, he navigated the twisted cable like a seasoned sailor. He crouched on a lone plank above them. "I believe that's my house you're on," he announced almost calmly. "Don't think it's going to hold long."

Ele attempted to stand but fell back in searing agony. Though hard to tell in the dark, she suspected her injuries were massive. She figured shock and floods of adrenaline must be dulling the pain.

Boone was reaching down for her.

Ele commanded, "Uncle Hoyt, take Boone's hand."

Uncle Hoyt reached up immediately. "Yes, Estus," he replied. Looking up at Boone, he announced, "If we go now, we won't miss dinner."

"Boone, take him. Take him!" ordered Ele.

Boone gripped Uncle Hoyt's forearm and heaved him up onto the bridge, making sure he had a firm grasp on the cable. Boone then crouched again, his hands extended.

"Now you, Ele!"

"I can't. I'm hurt. I think it's really bad."

"Ele! That house won't hold for two trips! Give me your hand. I can take you both right now!" Ele reached, then gasped at the wrenching pain in her side.

Boone searched frantically for an idea, his mind racing back over all the books he had read, all the places he had visited, all the things he had done. But there was nothing. He leaned out further over the ruined house in desperate hope.

Abruptly, the mass shifted, the bridge shuddered, and a staccato of "whip-twangs" sounded as cables began to snap. The roof section under Ele buckled and she plunged out of Boone's reach into the roiling framework.

"Ele!" Boone wailed.

"Boone!" Ele shouted firmly. "If you love me, take my Uncle Hoyt. Get him off that bridge before it falls, and then come back and get me. I won't leave you. I love you! We're getting married, remember?"

"Ele, please don't make me do this," Boone sobbed into the cold rain. "Don't make me choose. Please."

CHAPTER

12

"She was going to tell you today." – Uncle Hoyt

The morning was brilliant and blue. Uncle Hoyt was dressed in a charcoal gray well-tailored suit. He took hold of Ele and smiled down at her. Drawing a deep breath, he said, "Ready."

The pianist began playing as Arbuckle and Squirrel opened the two double doors. Hoyt escorted Ele down the aisle, step after measured step. The church was over-full, women in fine fancy hats and their best Sunday dresses nestled in the pews while their fine Appalachian-mannered men stood along the aisles. Every flat surface in the church was bedecked with flowers from well-wishers.

In the front stood Boone and Pastor Grant. Boone was magnificent in his new navy suit, a boutonniere of tiny white flowers in the lapel. His beard was close-trimmed, his unruly black hair freshly cut. He examined the large crowd of townsfolk, loved ones, and friends. Even Mike Wojcik and some members of Ele's firm sat just behind Boone's momma and daddy.

Boone's mind traveled back, yet again, to that night two weeks ago.

"Boone! Go!" Ele screamed out. Boone drew his fist back in an anguished clench. He turned, scooped up Hoyt, and scrambled across the ruined bridge. The instant their feet touched the bank's stable surface, Boone turned back toward Ele.

The bridge was gone, the mass was gone. The Subaru headlights flared across a raging, brown, empty river on the verge of cresting its banks. Boone screamed and struggled down the river's edge, tripping and sliding across drenched, tangled sawgrass and soup-like mud. Nothing. Nothing but water, rising, threatening, snapping at the embankments like a rabid cur. Boone fled up the hill and sank to his knees in the gravel road, his heart drowned in the water below.

The searchers found her the next day. Boone and Hoyt drove to the Shelton County Coroner's Office, viewed the body, and left in vacant shuffling silence. Boone heaved the truck door open and helped Hoyt up and in. Both men leaned back on the Ford's bench seat for a long time, staring at the polished granite steps of the county building.

"Boone..." Hoyt began, "I don't have any words. If I hadn't..."

Boone shook his head. "No, Doc, don't do that. Please don't. She's gone. I'm too tired to play the blame game right now. She's gone."

Boone put his forehead on the steering wheel. He sobbed suddenly, his knuckles white as he wept over them. "I had her, Hoyt, I had her." He looked at his hands grasping empty air. "She was right there, just a foot more reach and I could have grabbed her." His body collapsed like shattered pottery. Hoyt gathered Boone up against his shoulder and gripped him tight.

"There you go, son. No shame in it." Hoyt rocked him like a little boy. After a bit Boone straightened up and crushed his tears with the heel of his hand.

"I've got to tell you something now," Hoyt declared, "that Ele might not want me to tell you. But I have to. What I say isn't going to make things better – not by a long shot – but you have to hear it. Ele was sick, Boone. Really, really sick."

"What...do you mean, sick?" Boone's blotchy face stiffened.

"Mike Wojcik wasn't just Ele's former boyfriend, Boone. He was her oncologist." Boone tried to interrupt but Hoyt continued. "Son, Ele had a brain tumor. Secondary glioblastoma, diagnosed last year. Mike and his team tried all the available treatments, but it was Stage 4, invasive, particularly aggressive, and inoperable. She had only a handful of months to live.

"That's why the vomiting, the headaches, the dizziness – the tumor was growing rapidly and putting pressure on her brain. And it would have become much worse very soon: memory loss, maybe weakness on one side of her body, blindness, difficulty speaking, other possibilities depending on its location. It would have been awful."

"She never said..."

"She was going to tell you today," Hoyt said. He straightened his back and looked directly at Boone. "Now you listen, and listen good. That girl loved you, boy. She wanted to marry you, and to spend whatever time she had left with you.

"I know you're going to remember all these bitter days. I realize you can't just forget the brunt of them like most of us folks can. But you've got to take all the good memories and build up a wall around all the bad – close it off, lock it up, whatever you have to do so you can focus on the beauty that was Ele. Promise me, Son."

Hoyt reached the front of the church, stopped just shy of Boone, and nodded. Placing Ele's photograph on the lace-draped casket, he turned, hugged Boone, and followed him to the front pew. Pastor Grant began to speak.

"We are here today to remember a remarkable young lady, Elenora Estus Reese. Niece to our own beloved Hoyt and Estus Canby, friend of the Buchanan family" – he nodded to Anse, Bura, and Arbuckle and Squirrel who had just seated themselves from a side aisle – "and many others here, Elenora was a woman who has become very dear to all of us. "But we also come here to bear witness to a promise. It's a promise to be wed, made by two in the joy of love." Pastor Grant smiled at Boone, who struggled to keep his face calm. "Sadly, that day is not to be. Our time here is often fraught with tragedy and heartache, consequences of our humanity. When we weep, we weep in pain, in sorrow, in desperation, in anger.

"However, there are other tears: tears of joy, tears of happiness and laughter, and, most importantly, tears of love. So friends, when you leave here today, don't think of your tears for Elenora as evidence of your sorrow. Think of them as tears filled with joy, happiness, and jubilation that we had the privilege of knowing her, and also the hope of where our sister is today. And for you, Boone – hold onto that hope of reuniting with your beloved in the hereafter, and keep that love in your tears."

The church pianist played the first notes of "It Is Well," and the unmistakable tenor of Squirrel Buchanan soared like a song sparrow over the assembly. Heads turned to see him standing where he had been sitting.

> *When peace like a river, attendeth my way,*
> *When sorrows like sea billows roll*
> *Whatever my lot, Thou hast taught me to say*
> *It is well, it is well, with my soul.*

During the chorus, Arbuckle got up and added a perfect harmony. By the second verse, everyone was standing to join the song.

The service concluded with the congregation shuffling past Boone and Hoyt with damp eyes, awkward condolences, sweet memories, and tissue-gripped hugs.

After a short graveside service at the Buchanan family plot,

Hoyt invited the townsfolk up to the Wayah Inn. The Town Square Cafe was closed, of course, so a caterer was hired from Asheville. The upper pasture, now dry, clear, and removed of cattle and their leavings, served for parking. The porch and front lawn were crowded with tables, chairs, and small huddles of people overdressed for the hot September afternoon.

Uncle Hoyt sat in a lawn chair overlooking the proceedings, Boone beside him in a dining room chair. Tall jars of sweet tea were sweating on a plastic folding table. Folks came over to offer comfort or swap a silence-filling story, and both men nodded and smiled tiredly, unsure how to act.

Arbuckle and Squirrel approached, Bura between them. Anse, visibly uncomfortable in an over-sized gray suit, limped behind them, using a folding chair as a makeshift cane. He unfolded the chair and settled it on the grass for his wife. Once their momma was seated, Arbuckle and Squirrel nodded to the two men. "Be back directly," Arbuckle told Hoyt.

Bura spoke. "Boone tells us you put the word in for him at Tennessee to go to veternary school. That was right nice of you."

"The department head is a fraternity brother of mine," Uncle Hoyt explained. "He said as soon as Boone takes the GED at ABTech, they'll process his application. But really, what sold Boone was Boone himself. Once I told my friend the skills and training Boone already had, he was chomping at the bit to meet our boy. Now mind you, UT is no University of Pennsylvania," he added with a mock-serious face. "But it's only two hours away, so I guess it'll do."

"Well, we thank you. We also 'preciate you lettin' us stay here at the Inn. We'll do right by you," Bura said as she patted Hoyt's hand, "but I ain't gonna put up with your nekkid carry'n on, that's for damn sure."

"Whatever you say, Bura," Hoyt replied, chuckling. "Anything to get Buchanan cooking and moonshine in my house on a regular basis."

They chatted about college and small anecdotes of Ele. The sun settled just above the ridge, and autumn cool finally began to seep along the riverbed.

Awhile later, just as dusk began washing out the day's colors, Arbuckle and Squirrel came back around the house and pushed their way between Boone and Hoyt. Squirrel plopped a small cardboard box on the small table next to Hoyt.

"Open it," said Arbuckle.

Confused, Uncle Hoyt looked over at Boone, who shrugged his shoulders. Hoyt lifted the box lid and a golden ball of fur popped up. A fluffy, peach-colored puppy poured out of the box and tumbled into Hoyt's lap, jumping up to immediately lick his clean-shaven face. Hoyt laughed uproariously.

"Squirrel found her at Momma's cafe a couple of days ago," Arbuckle explained. "She ain't got no ma we could find, but I'm pretty dang sure who her daddy is," he laughed. "I hope you don't mind, we named her Apricot."

"Apricot?" Hoyt cried, lifting the puppy to look in her eyes. "Are you an Apricot? Yeah, I guess you are." He scruffed the puppy, felt her legs and torso, flipped her ears back in an absent-minded examination. Then he pronounced her healthy and placed her back on the table to wander around the paper plates and cups.

After the puppy had lapped up enough leftover cake and squash casserole, she wiggled over to Anse sitting alone at the far end of the table. Surprisingly, he picked up the pup and tucked her between his arms, where she fell soundly asleep.

Boone walked out onto the porch. All the visitors had gone home, and the quiet clatter of cleanup drifted from the kitchen.

He looked out over the river, night just touching its banks and the lonely pylons that once held the footbridge. The sight of them brought sorrow and longing, like a punch to the chest. But he was determined to focus on only the good memories of Ele: big blue eyes, a head of golden curls, a stunning red dress, a deep, deep kiss.

There were also today's new memories and images to help him weather the pain. His momma's smile when Squirrel and Arbuckle sang that glorious hymn. Anse scratching his neck in that new dress shirt. Pastor Grant's strong hug promising support in the coming days. And the image just now, of a glowing lantern across the pasture carried by an old white-haired naked man, leading a little peach-colored puppy.

THE END

About the Writer

Nathaniel Embers, the fictional alter-ego of Jon Frank of the Web series When Fact Met Fiction is actually award-winning writer David W. Rogers.

A native of the Blue Ridge Mountains in Western North Carolina, David W. Rogers has been a storyteller since he learned to talk. When he was only six years old, his Uncle Charlie would pay him a quarter a story just to hear the yarns he would spin.

Returning to college following over twenty years in the work force, David completed a BA in Literature at University of North Carolina at Asheville in 2013.

David has written five plays performed in local venues, as well as dozens of short stories. One of those stories, "Honeydew," won the 2013 Thomas Wolfe Award for Short Fiction.

The Love In Our Tears is David's first novel, and a slight departure from his usual genre, Appalachian fantasy fiction. His next venture, Haint Blue, a collection of short stories, will be available in digital and print formats in early 2017.

David is a veteran of the US Army, husband of Madalyn, and father of four children. He's also "Giddy" to two grandchildren. In addition to writing, he loves spending time with family, reading, collecting board games, and driving in the snow.

whenfactmetfiction.com

www.ingramcontent.com/pod-product-compliance
Lightning Source LLC
Chambersburg PA
CBHW021844090426

42811CB00033B/2136/J